First World War

and Army of Occupation

War Diary

France, Belgium and Germany

40 DIVISION
120 Infantry Brigade
King's Own (Yorkshire Light Infantry)
15th Battalion
1 March 1918 - 6 June 1919

WO95/2612/2

The Naval & Military Press Ltd
www.nmarchive.com
Published in association with The National Archives

Published by

The Naval & Military Press Ltd

Unit 10 Ridgewood Industrial Park,

Uckfield, East Sussex,

TN22 5QE England

Tel: +44 (0) 1825 749494

www.naval-military-press.com

www.nmarchive.com

This diary has been reprinted in facsimile from the original. Any imperfections are inevitably reproduced and the quality may fall short of modern type and cartographic standards.

© Crown Copyright
Images reproduced by permission of The National Archives, London, England, 2015.

Contents

Document type	Place/Title	Date From	Date To
Heading	WO95/2612 (2)		
Heading	40th Division 120th Infy Bde 15th Bn K.O.Y.L.I. Jun 1918-Jun 1919		
Heading	War Diary Of 15th (Garr) Bn K.O.Y.L.I. From 10th June 1918 To 30th June 1918 (Inclusive)		
War Diary	Etaples	10/06/1918	10/06/1918
War Diary	Buysscheure	11/06/1918	23/06/1918
War Diary	La Belle Hotesse	24/06/1918	30/06/1918
Operation(al) Order(s)	15th (G) Battn Kings Own yorks Light Infantry. Order No. 1	16/06/1918	16/06/1918
Miscellaneous	Administrative Instructions Occupation Of W. Hazebrouck Line		
Miscellaneous	Amendment to Administrative Instructions-Occupation of W Hazebrouck Line		
Miscellaneous	15th Garrison Battalion, Kings Gun Yorkshire Light Infantry. Defence Of Battalion Sector.	21/06/1918	21/06/1918
Miscellaneous	Headquarters 120th Infantry Brigade Weekly Report In Training		
Operation(al) Order(s)	15th (G) Battalion Kings Own Yorkshire Light Infantry Order No. 2	22/06/1918	22/06/1918
Operation(al) Order(s)	To Accompany 15th K.O.Y.L.I.-Order No. 2		
Miscellaneous	Headquarters 120th Infantry Brigade Weekly Report On Training		
Operation(al) Order(s)	15th Battalion King's Gun Yorkshire Light Infantry Order No. 3	26/06/1918	26/06/1918
War Diary	La Belle Hotesse	01/07/1918	09/07/1918
War Diary	Le Romarin	10/07/1918	31/07/1918
Miscellaneous	Report By Maj Gen. Commdg. 40th Division 120th Inf. Brigade. Appendix I		
Miscellaneous	15th Battalion Kings Own Yorkshire Light Infantry.	11/07/1918	11/07/1918
Operation(al) Order(s)	15th Battalion King's Gun Yorkshire Light Infantry Order No. 6	01/08/1918	01/08/1918
Heading	Officer i/c A.G's Office, At The Base.		
Heading	15th Battalion King's Gun Yorkshire Light Infantry War Diary 1st-31st August 1918		
War Diary	La Belle Hotesse	01/08/1918	02/08/1918
War Diary	Lumbres	03/08/1918	07/08/1918
War Diary	La Belle Hotesse	08/08/1918	11/08/1918
War Diary	Le Tir Anglais	12/08/1918	12/08/1918
War Diary	Aval Wood	13/08/1918	13/08/1918
War Diary	Front Line	14/08/1918	17/08/1918
War Diary	Le Tir Anglais	18/08/1918	20/08/1918
War Diary	Aval Wood	21/08/1918	31/08/1918
Operation(al) Order(s)	Administrative Instructions Move 2nd August 1918. To Accompany 15th Battalion. K.O.Y.L.I. Order No. 6	01/08/1918	01/08/1918
Heading	War Diary		
Miscellaneous	15th Battalion King's Own Yorkshire Light Infantry. Appendix No 2	07/08/1918	07/08/1918
Miscellaneous	File		

Operation(al) Order(s)	Operation Order No. 7 By Lieut Col. T.W.T. Isaac Commanding 15th Battalion Kings Own Yorkshire Light Infantry.	10/08/1918	10/08/1918
Heading	War Diary.		
Operation(al) Order(s)	15th Battalion K.O.Y.L.I. Relief Order No. 1 By Lieut. Col. T.W.T. Isaac Commanding	12/08/1918	12/08/1918
Operation(al) Order(s)	15th Battalion. K.O.Y.L.I. Relief Order No. 2 By Lieut. Colonel. I.W.J. Isaac. Commdg. Appendix No 4	13/08/1918	13/08/1918
Heading	War Diary		
Miscellaneous	15th Battalion, King's Own Yorkshire Light. Infantry Account Of Operations From 13th August To 29th August 1918. Appendix No 5	13/08/1918	13/08/1918
Operation(al) Order(s)	15th Battalion, King's Own Yorkshire Light. Infantry Order No 3 By Lieut Colonel T.W.T. Isaac Commanding.	16/08/1918	16/08/1918
Heading	War Diary		
Miscellaneous	O.C.	16/08/1918	16/08/1918
Miscellaneous	Battalion in Forward Gone And Z Line. 15th Battalion K.O.Y.L.I. Defence Orders Appendix No 7	16/08/1918	16/08/1918
Operation(al) Order(s)	15th Battalion Kings Own Yorkshire Light Infantry Order No. 7 By Right Colonel T.W.T. Isaac Appendix No 8	22/08/1918	22/08/1918
Heading	War Diary		
Miscellaneous	Appendix No 9		
Miscellaneous	120th Infantry Brigade Intelligence Summary Right Sector.	24/08/1918	24/08/1918
War Diary	Appendix No II		
Operation(al) Order(s)	Appendix No 12 15th Battalion Kings Own Yorkshire Light Infantry Order No 8. By Lieut. Col. T.W.T. Isaac Commanding.	24/08/1918	24/08/1918
Map	War Diary		
Operation(al) Order(s)	15th Battalion Kings Own Yorkshire Light Infantry Order No. 9. By Lieut. Col. T.W.T. Isaac Commanding.	26/08/1919	26/08/1919
Miscellaneous			
Miscellaneous	Appendix No 13		
Miscellaneous	Appendix No 15		
Operation(al) Order(s)	15th Battalion Kings Own Yorkshire Light Infantry Order No 10 By Lieut. Col. T.W.T. Isaac Commanding	26/08/1918	26/08/1918
Miscellaneous	War Diary		
Miscellaneous	15th Battalion King's Own. Yorkshire Light Infantry Amendments To Order No. 10	26/08/1918	26/08/1918
Miscellaneous	Appendix No 18		
Miscellaneous	Appendix 19	28/08/1918	28/08/1918
Operation(al) Order(s)	15th Battalion King's Own Yorkshire Light Infantry Order No. II By Lt. Col T.W.T. Isaac Commanding	28/08/1918	28/08/1918
Miscellaneous	War Diary		
Miscellaneous	Appendix No 21		
Miscellaneous	40th Division No. 901 (A). Appendix No 22	28/08/1918	28/08/1918
Operation(al) Order(s)	15th Battalion King's Own Yorkshire Light Infantry. Order No. 12 By Major H.J.R. Bock, Commanding.	30/08/1918	30/08/1918
Miscellaneous	Dear Col Isaacs	23/08/1918	23/08/1918
Miscellaneous	Appendix No 24		
Miscellaneous	Copy Certificate	22/08/1918	22/08/1918
Miscellaneous	A Form. Messages And Signals.		
Heading	15 Koyli Vol 3		

Heading	War Diary of 15th Battalion K.O.Y.L.I. From 1st September 1918 To 30th September 1918 Volume (IV) Vol 4		
Heading	War Diary of 15th Battalion K.O.Y.L.I. From 1st September 1918 To 30th September 1918 Volume IV		
War Diary	Wallon Cappell	01/09/1918	11/09/1918
War Diary	Lupin Farm	12/09/1918	13/09/1918
War Diary	Poston Farm	14/09/1918	15/09/1918
War Diary	Hollebeque Farm	16/09/1918	16/09/1918
War Diary	Taffy Farm	17/09/1918	19/09/1918
War Diary	Lett Farm	20/09/1918	23/09/1918
War Diary	Le Verrier	24/09/1918	27/09/1918
War Diary	Padoy Farm	28/09/1918	30/09/1918
Miscellaneous	Battalion Order By Major H.J.R. Book Commanding 15th Battalion King's Own Yorkshire Light Infantry.	03/09/1918	03/09/1918
Miscellaneous	15th Battalion King's Own Yorkshire Light Infantry. Order No. 18 By Major H.J.R. Book Commanding.	26/02/1918	26/02/1918
Miscellaneous	War Diary		
Operation(al) Order(s)	15th Battalion King's Own Yorkshire Light Infantry. Operation Order No. 15. Major H.J.R. Bock Commanding. Appendix III	13/09/1918	13/09/1918
Miscellaneous			
Operation(al) Order(s)	Cavalry, Artillery And Infantry Only.		
Miscellaneous	1st Battalion King's Own Yorkshire Right Infantry Defence Instructions No. 1 Major H.J.R. Bock Commanding	18/09/1918	18/09/1918
Miscellaneous			
Operation(al) Order(s)	15th Battalion King's Own Yorkshire Light Infantry. Operation Order No. 17 By Major H.J.R. Bock Commanding.	19/09/1918	19/09/1918
Miscellaneous			
Operation(al) Order(s)	15th Battalion King's Own Yorkshire Light Infantry. Operation Order No. 18. by Captain. T.L. Webb. Commanding. Appendix VII	21/09/1918	21/09/1918
Miscellaneous			
Miscellaneous	Battalion Orders by Major L.M. Sandison, Commanding 15th Battalion King's Own Yorkshire Light Infantry.	27/09/1918	27/09/1918
Miscellaneous			
Heading	War Diary of 15th Bn. Kings Own Yorkshire Light Infantry From 1st October 1918 To 31st October 1918 Volume No. 5		
Miscellaneous			
War Diary	Nieppe	01/10/1918	04/10/1918
War Diary	Armentieres	05/10/1918	09/10/1918
War Diary	Erquingham	10/10/1918	12/10/1918
War Diary	E of Steenwarck	13/10/1918	16/10/1918
War Diary	Rue Marle	17/10/1918	17/10/1918
War Diary	Champreulle	18/10/1918	18/10/1918
War Diary	Wambrechies	18/10/1918	19/10/1918
War Diary	St Andre	20/10/1918	22/10/1918
War Diary	St. Andre	23/09/1918	27/09/1918
War Diary	Lannoy	28/09/1918	01/11/1918
Operation(al) Order(s)	15th Battalion King's Own Yorkshire Light Infantry. Operation Order No. 20. By Major L.M. By Sandison Commanding. Appendix I	01/10/1918	01/10/1918

Operation(al) Order(s)	Order No. 21 By Lt. Col. T.W.T. Isaac, Commanding 15th Battalion King's Own Yorkshire Light Infantry. Appendix II	05/10/1918	05/10/1918
Miscellaneous			
Operation(al) Order(s)	Operation Order No. 22 By Lt. Col. T.W.T. Isaac. Commanding "N" Battalion King's Own Yorkshire Light Infantry	09/10/1918	09/10/1918
Operation(al) Order(s)	15th Battalion King's Own Yorkshire Light Infantry Order No. 23 By Lieut. Colonel T.W.T. Isaac Commanding. Appendix IV	12/10/1918	12/10/1918
Miscellaneous	Special Order of The Day by Major-General Sir W.E. Peyton, K.C.B., K.C.V.O., D.S.O., Commanding 40th Division. Appendix V	19/10/1918	19/10/1918
Miscellaneous			
Operation(al) Order(s)	15th Battalion K.O.Y.L.I. Match Order No. 1 Appendix VI	27/10/1918	27/10/1918
Miscellaneous	Release From The Army For Coal-Mining (Overseas)		
Miscellaneous	Battalion Orders by Captain T.L. Webb Commanding 15th Battalion King's Own Yorkshire Light Infantry. Appendix VII	29/10/1918	29/10/1918
Miscellaneous	Release From The Army For Coal-Mining (Overseas).		
Miscellaneous			
Miscellaneous	Armee Belge. Chef d' Etat-Major General	03/10/1918	03/10/1918
Miscellaneous	120th Inf. Bde. No. 120/429 Appendix VIII	08/10/1918	08/10/1918
Heading	War Diary of 15th Battalion K.O.Y.L.I. For The Month of November 1918 Volume No. VI		
Miscellaneous			
War Diary	Lannoy	01/11/1918	06/11/1918
War Diary	Nechin	07/11/1918	09/11/1918
War Diary	Herinnes	10/11/1918	12/11/1918
War Diary	Bucquoy	13/11/1918	28/11/1918
Miscellaneous	Battalion Orders by Captain T.L. Webb Commanding 15th Battalion King's Own Yorkshire Light Infantry. Appendix I		
Miscellaneous	Release From The Army For Coal-Mining (Overseas)		
Miscellaneous			
Miscellaneous	Release From The Army For Coal-Mining (Overseas)		
Miscellaneous	15th Battalion King's Own Yorkshire Light Infantry Appendix II	04/11/1918	04/11/1918
Operation(al) Order(s)	15th. Battn. K.O.Y.L.I. March Order No. 2 Appendix III	05/11/1918	05/11/1918
Miscellaneous	M.O		
Miscellaneous	Battalion Orders by Captain T.L. Webb. Commanding 15th Battalion King's Own Yorkshire Light Infantry Appendix IV	08/11/1918	08/11/1918
Miscellaneous			
Miscellaneous	Training		
Miscellaneous	Release From The Army For Coal-Mining (Overseas)		
Operation(al) Order(s)	15th Battalion K.O.Y.L.I. March Order No. 3 Appendix V	09/11/1918	09/11/1918
Miscellaneous	Release From The Army For Coal-Mining (Overseas)		
Miscellaneous	Battalion Orders by Lieut.-Colonel T.W.T. Isaac. Commanding 15th Battalion King's Own Yorkshire Light Infantry.	11/11/1918	11/11/1918
Miscellaneous			

Operation(al) Order(s)	15th Battalion K.O.Y.L.I. March Order No. 4 Appendix VII		
Miscellaneous			
Miscellaneous	Battalion Orders. by Lieut. Colonel T.W.T. Isaac. Commanding 15th Battalion King's Own Yorkshire Light Infantry.	14/11/1918	14/11/1918
Miscellaneous			
Miscellaneous	Release From The Army For Coal-Mining (Overseas)		
Miscellaneous	Battalion Orders by Lieut-Colonel T.W.T. Isaac, Commanding 15th Battalion King's Own Yorkshire Light Infantry. Appendix IX	14/11/1918	14/11/1918
Miscellaneous			
Miscellaneous	Battalion Orders by Lieut-Colonel T.W.T. Isaac, Commanding 15th Battalion King's Own Yorkshire Light Infantry.	15/11/1918	15/11/1918
Miscellaneous	Release From The Army For Coal-Mining (Overseas)		
Miscellaneous			
Miscellaneous	Battalion Orders, by Lieut-Colonel T.W.T. Isaac, Commanding 15th Battalion King's Own Yorkshire Light Infantry	16/11/1918	16/11/1918
Miscellaneous			
Miscellaneous	Battalion Orders by Lieut. Colonel T.W.T. Isaac, Commanding 15th Battalion King's Own Yorkshire Infantry. Appendix XII	17/11/1918	17/11/1918
Miscellaneous			
Miscellaneous	Battalion Orders by Lieut-Colonel T.W.T. Isaac, Commanding 16th Battalion King's Own Yorkshire Light Infantry.	13/11/1918	13/11/1918
Miscellaneous			
Miscellaneous	Release From The Army For Coal-Mining (Overseas)		
Miscellaneous	Battalion Order by Lieut-Colonel T.W.T. Isaac, Commanding 15th Battn. King's Own Yorkshire Light Infantry. Appendix XIV	19/11/1918	19/11/1918
Miscellaneous	Release From The Army For Coal-Mining (Overseas)		
Miscellaneous			
Miscellaneous	Release From The Army For Coal-Mining (Overseas)		
Miscellaneous	Battalion Orders by Major T.L. Webb Commanding 15th Battalion King's Own Yorkshire Light Infantry. Appendix XV	23/11/1918	23/11/1918
Miscellaneous	Battalion Orders by Major T.L. Webb Commanding 15th Battalion King's Own Yorkshire Light Infantry Appendix XVI	26/11/1918	26/11/1918
Miscellaneous			
Heading	War Diary of 15th Bn K.O.Y.L.I. For The Month of December 1918 Vol7		
Miscellaneous			
War Diary	Toufflers	01/03/1918	31/03/1918
Heading	War Diary of 15th Bn. K.O.Y.L.I. For January 1919 Vol 8		
Miscellaneous			
War Diary	Toufflers	01/01/1919	31/01/1919
Miscellaneous	Brigade Routine Order by Brigadier General The Hon. W.R. Hore Ruthven, C.M.g. D.S.O. Commanding 120th Infantry Brigade.	04/01/1919	04/01/1919
Heading	War Diary of For The Month of February 1919 of 15th Bn K.O.Y.L.I.		

Miscellaneous			
War Diary	Toufflers	01/02/1919	28/02/1919
Miscellaneous	D.A.G.	07/06/1919	07/06/1919
War Diary	Croix	01/05/1919	06/06/1919

WO95/2612 (2)

WO95/2612 (2)

40TH DIVISION
120TH INFY BDE

15TH BN K.O.Y.L.I.

JUN 1918-JUN 1919

Formed June 1918

1A

WAR DIARY

OF

15th (GARR) Bn K.O.Y.L.I

FROM

10th JUNE 1918

TO

30th JUNE 1918

(INCLUSIVE)

Army Form C. 2118.

WAR DIARY
~~or~~
~~INTELLIGENCE SUMMARY.~~
(Erase heading not required.)

Instructions regarding War Diaries and Intelligence Summaries are contained in F. S. Regs., Part II. and the Staff Manual respectively. Title pages will be prepared in manuscript.

Place	Date	Hour	Summary of Events and Information	Remarks and references to Appendices
ETAPLES	10/6/18		The C.O. 2nd in Command, Adjutant, Transport Officer Quarter master, and H. Qrs. Coy of 100 N.C.O.s & men more or less of this new Battalion (named the 10th Garrison Bn) entrained at ETAPLES, detrained at WATTEN, and marched to BUYSSCHEURE where the Bn was to be organised. The march of about 10 Kilometers was accomplished without anyone falling out, which was creditable considering that the men with few exceptions, were of Category B i and B ii, and all carried full Packs, ground sheets and Blankets. After arrival at BUYSSCHEURE, the name of the Bn. was changed to the 15th (Garr.) Bn K.O.Y.L.I. The following are the names of the original officers at H. Qrs.– C.O. Lieut Col. F.C. McCordick 2nd in Comnd Major J. RALSTON BOCK T.D. Adj: Capt. L.M. SANDISON Asst. Adj. Lieut. J. W. SWANSON TRANS.t officer Capt. A. LINDEMERE, Quarter Master Lieut F. NUNLEY M.O. Capt. C H. CARROLL	JRB
BUYSSCHEURE	11/6/18		abt. 11-30 p.m. Officers, N.C.O.s and men, numbering 700 or thereby arrived from different Labour Bns to complete the strength of the Bn. These men are almost entirely all of Category B i & B ii (certified not fit to march more than 5 miles.)	JRB

D. D. & L., London, E.C. (A8004) Wt. W1771/M2 31 750,000 5/17 Sch. 52 Forms/C2118/14

Instructions regarding War Diaries and Intelligence Summaries are contained in F. S. Regs., Part II. and the Staff Manual respectively. Title pages will be prepared in manuscript.

WAR DIARY

~~or~~

~~INTELLIGENCE SUMMARY~~.

(*Erase heading not required.*)

Army Form C. 2118.

Place	Date	Hour	Summary of Events and Information	Remarks and references to Appendices
BUYSSCHEURE	12/6/18 13/6/18		Occupied in organising, and re-equipping N.C.O.s and men	JRB JRB.
	14/6/18		Started training	JRB.
	15/6/18		The Bn. was inspected by the G.O.C 40th Division, Maj. Gen J. PONSONBY C.B. CMG D.S.O. He expressed himself as being pleased with the appearance of the men	JRB.
	16/6/18 Sunday		The C.O. 2nd in Comnd. & Coy. Commanders reconnoitred the W. HAZEBROUCK trench line in the LA ROMARIN area, were conveyed there & back by Motor Bus	Appendices I - IV JRB
	17/6/18		The 40th DIV. transferred to 15th Corps	JRB.
	18/6/18		TRAINING.	JRB Appendix IVA
	19/6/18		Bn. inspected by the D.A.G.	JRB
	20/6/18 21/6/18		TRAINING The Bn. officers held first mess dinner	JRB JRB
	22/6/18		Orders received to move on 23rd inst to LA BELLE HOTESSE	JRB.

D. D. & L., London, E.C. (A8004) Wt. W1771/M2-31 750,000 5/17 Sch. 52 Forms/C2118/14

Instructions regarding War Diaries and Intelligence Summaries are contained in F. S. Regs., Part II. and the Staff Manual respectively. Title pages will be prepared in manuscript.

WAR DIARY

~~or~~

~~INTELLIGENCE SUMMARY.~~

(Erase heading not required.)

Army Form C. 2118.

Place	Date	Hour	Summary of Events and Information	Remarks and references to Appendices
BUYSSCHEURE	23/6/18 Sunday		Left for LA BELLE HOTESSE Marched to em-bussing point Some men fell out. Marched from de-bussing point to Camp No men fell out. Accommodated in tents & bivouacs	appendices V - VI JKB
LA BELLE HOTESSE	24/6/18		TRAINING as per programme	JKB
	25/6/18		Manned the Bn sector of W. HAZEBROUCK line of trenches Brig. Gen. HOBKIRK Comdg the 120th Bgde, inspected the Bn dispositions C.O. laid up with SPANISH FLU & temperature. Several officers & a number of men suffering from the same complaint	JKB
	26/6/18		TRAINING	JKB appendix VIA
	27/6/18		2nd in Comnd with Officers & N.C.O's of the 3 Labour Coys attached to the Bn as reserves visited the W HAZEBROUCK trench line and selected positions for these reserve Coys. The Labour Coys attached are named as follows, & will occupy positions as stated, — 84th Labour Coy in trenches on right of Bn H. Qrs. 92nd do do in rear do do 110th do do on left do do	JKB

D. D. & L., London, E.C.
(A8004) Wt. W1771/M2-31 750,000 5/17 Sch. 52 Forms/C2118/14

Instructions regarding War Diaries and Intelligence Summaries are contained in F. S. Regs., Part II. and the Staff Manual respectively. Title pages will be prepared in manuscript.

WAR DIARY

or

~~INTELLIGENCE SUMMARY.~~

(*Erase heading not required.*)

Army Form C. 2118.

Place	Date	Hour	Summary of Events and Information	Remarks and references to Appendices
LA BELLE HOTESSE	28/6/18		The Bn again occupied their sector of W. HAZEBROUCK trench line. C.O. altered dispositions & put 3 coys (instead of 2 coys) in front line	Appendix XVII gkB
	29/6/18		The M.O. Capt. C.H. CARROLL, left to fill another appointment. His successor, Capt. J.M. RYAN arriving. Training as per programme. 10 new officers arrived	gkB
	30/6/18 Sunday		First Bn Football match played – R & S coys v. Q & T coys – (R & S coys owing to sickness of members of team, unable at last moment to play – Q & T coys team played scratch team.)	gkB

30-6-18.

F. H. McCordick Lt-Col.
Comdg 15th KOYLI

D. D. & L., London, E.C.
(A8004) Wt. W1771/M2731 750,000 5/17 Sch 52 Forms/C2118/14

SECRET

I

COPY NO. 3

15th (S) Battn Kings Own Yorks Light Infantry. Order No 1.

16th June 1918.

Ref maps.
Sheet 36 A.
Sketch.

1. In the event of an enemy attack on the II Army front the 120th Brigade and attached troops will man the WEST HAZEBROUCK Line from D 25 c in the South to C 12 b in the North.

2. The following troops will be attached to 15th K.O.Y.L.I. in the event of the line being manned:

94 Labour Coy - strength about 30 Officers and 350 O.R.
Present Location - C 22 d 6.5.

The men are at present untrained.

3. The 120th Brigade sector will be divided up into 3 sections, of which the southern one will be held by the 10th K.O.S.B: the centre by 15th K.O.Y.L.I: and the northern by the 11th Cameron Highlanders, each with attached troops.

4. The Battalion will proceed from billets to the vicinity of the trench system by busses, details of which will be issued later.

5. The Battalion sector will be as follows:

Right Outpost Coy - "R" Coy from D 19 a 2.1. to point where trench crosses road (road inclusive) at D 13 c Central.

Left Outpost Coy - "Q" Coy from D 13 c Central to C 17 b 2.9.

Right Support Coy - "T" Coy in trenches about D 13 c 0.2.

Left Support Coy - "S" Coy in trenches about C 18 b 5.2.

Reserve - 94 Labour Coy at C 17 c 7.7.

Battalion Hd Qrs. will be in farm at C 17 c 3.9.

Regtl Aid Post near Bn Hd. Qrs.

6. Commanders of Outpost Coys are responsible for liaison with Outpost Coys on their respective flanks.

7. It must be impressed upon all ranks that they are to hold the Line in which they are posted, whether it be the Outpost Line or Line of Resistance, to the last man and the last round of ammunition. No withdrawal of troops will take place, even from the Line of Observation, unless orders are received from Battn Headquarters.

8. The following will be carried to the trenches:

120 rounds of S.A.A. on each man.
2000 " per Lewis Gun.
{1 days rations and
{1 iron ration on each man.

Water bottles will be filled, and rifle magazines loaded.

9. Company Commanders will prepare a scheme for the occupation of their section. These will be forwarded to the Orderly Room as early as possible.

10. This is precautionary order and will come into effect only on the word "Move".

(sgd) L. M. Sanderson
Capt. & Adj.
15th K.O.Y.L.I.

SECRET II Copy No. 3.

Administrative Instructions Occupation of W. HAZEBROUCK Line

Ref Map 1/40000
Sheets 27
36A.

Reference 15th Batt. R.W.F. Order No. 1 dated 16-6-18

1.(a) The Battalion will proceed to the line by lorries embussing at LEDERZEELE cross roads, head of column facing North, at G 27 c 8.0, and will debus at LA BELLE HOTESSE or SERCUS.

(b) Approximate embussing strength will be sent to Orderly Room as soon as possible.

(c) If lorries are not available the Battn will proceed by march route.

2. Surplus Kit.

(a) Officers kits and mess boxes, blankets (tightly rolled in bundles of 10 and labelled) and any other stores not absolutely essential for fighting, will be dumped at the Quartermasters Stores.

(b) O.C. "[illegible]" Coy will detail a guard of 1 N.C.O. and 3 men for this dump. The guard will be provided with two days rations, and on departure of the Battn the N.C.O. in charge will report to Area Commandant LEDERZEELE regarding further orders.

(c) Dress — full marching order.

3. Transport. Battn Transport lines and Q.M. Stores will be situated at approximately [illegible] (Sheet 36a). Orders for move of transport will be issued later.

4. 23 Lewis Guns per Coy and 8 per Battn H.Q. will be filled and dumped in Transport lines. The Transport Officer will convey them to the [illegible] where they will be drawn by Coys, [illegible] them.

5. Rations. [illegible]

- 2 -

6. Ammunition. In addition to the S.A.A. already issued, a Battalion reserve of 50,000 rounds will be maintained. The Transport Officer will arrange to take this forward to the Lines.

7. Brigade S.A.A. Dump. Two G.S. Baggage Wagons after arrival at Transport Lines will be attached under orders from Brigade H.Q. for conveyance of S.A.A. from Supply Refilling Point to Brigade S.A.A. Dump. The Transport Officer will arrange to take S.A.A. forward from Brigade Dump to Battn Dumps (if possible). Any available transport of 9th Labour Coy will be used for this purpose under the orders of the Transport Officer.

8. Medical Arrangements. An Advanced Dressing Station is being established at C.2.c.3.9 ([illegible]). O.C. 9th Labour Coy will detail 30 men from the unarmed personnel to report to the above A.D.S. for duty as stretcher bearers.

9. Lewis Guns. The Transport Officer will arrange to collect all Lewis Guns and magazines from Coys and convey them to the Lines.

10. Stretchers. The stretchers at present in possession of each Coy will be taken.

(Signed) [illegible]
Capt and Adjt
13th Serv Battn, K.O.Y.L.I.

Copies to all recipients of Order No 1.

SECRET

III

COPY NO. 4

Amendments to Administrative Instruction – Occupation of W HAZEBROUCK Line

6 (b) Battalion Reserve of 50,000 rounds will be carried in limbered G S wagons of First Line Transport of Battalions. Lewis Gun Reserve of 32,000 rounds in limbered G S wagons or G S Baggage wagons. The Transport Officer will collect Lewis Guns and full magazines from Companies and convey them to the Lorries where Companies will draw their own guns etc. and take them in their lorries.

8 (a) The 33 men from 9th Labour Coy. will be detailed by O.C. 6th Labour Group.

(sgd) L M Sandison
Capt & Adj.
15th (S) Battn KOYLI.

Copies to all recipients of above instructions.

War Diary.

IV

SECRET

15th Garrison Battalion, King's Own Yorkshire Light Infantry

Defence of Battalion Sector.

Ref. Order No 1 and Administrative Instructions

Action will be taken as follows :-

1. If the enemy penetrates our front line.

Support companies will counter-attack, if necessary, under orders of Company Commanders.

They will not move up as reinforcements for front line without orders from Battalion Headquarters.

Reserve Coys. will act only under orders from Battalion Headquarters.

2. If the enemy penetrates the front line of either unit on our flanks:

A counter attack from the flanks will be promptly delivered under Orders of O.C. support Coy concerned. The other support Coy. will extend its front as soon as it is known that the first Coy. is attacking to a flank.

Reserve Coys. will act only under orders from Battalion Headquarters.

(Signed) F.C. McCordick Lt. Col
Commanding 15th Garr. Battalion, K.O.Y.L.I.

21-6-18.

Copies to all recipients of Order No 1.

To/ Headquarters,
120th. Infantry Brigade

IV A

Weekly Report on Training

I beg to report as follows on the progress in training of this Battalion:

Musketry. Progress has been made in the elementary stages, but lack of a range and of dummy ammunition has prevented more advanced training being carried out.

Lewis Gun. Each team has received several hours' instruction from Corps School Instructors, who report favourably on their progress. This refers to one team per platoon.

Physical Training. This also shows improvement; but there are a number of men who appear unlikely to reach a good standard of physical fitness.

Gas. Particular attention has been paid to this branch of training, and a fair standard of efficiency has been reached.

Other Branches. Signallers are undergoing instruction at Corps School. Bombing instruction has not been given this week.

General. The training of Officers is being carried out by means of lectures, exercises etc.

Lt.-Col.
Commanding
15th. Bn, K.O.Y.L.I.

SECRET

V

COPY NO 4

15th (S) Battalion Kings Own Yorkshire Light Infantry.

Order NO 2

maps. HAZEBROUCK 5.A.
Sheet 27
Sheet 36 A.

22.6.18.

O

1. The Battalion will move to area West of LA BELLE HOTESSE tomorrow, 23rd inst.

2. The Battalion will assemble at M.6.a.7.9. ready to move off. at 7.0 a.m. Dress Full marching order, steel helmets at back of packs. Order of march - Q.R.S.T. Coys, H.Q. Qrs.

3. The Battalion will march to LEDERZEELE - ST MOMELIN Road (G.33 c.79) and will embuss there at 8.0 a.m.

4. The 1st Line Transport will be brigaded and will move to new area under Captain TRITTON. 10th Batt K.O.S.B. Head of column to pass starting point (OOST HOUCK Church) at 9.30 a.m.

(Sgd) L. M. Sandison
Capt. & adj.
15th (S) Batt KOYLI.

Copy NO. 1. to C.O.
" " 2. " Adjutant
" " 3 " War Diary
" " 4 " File
" " 5 " Q Coy
" " 6 " R "
" " 7 " S "
" " 8 " T "
" " 9 " Q.M.
" " 10 " M.O.
" " 11 " T.O.
" " 12 " R.S.M.
" " 13 " 120th Brigade.

File

~~VI~~ O File

To accompany 15th K.O.Y.L.I. Order No. 2

1 Accomodation. The Battalion will be accomodated in tented camps and available billets at [illegible] C 14 d 5 0

2 Blankets, officers' kits, mess boxes, Lewis guns and equipment and all Coy stores will be dumped by Companies on a main road by 6·0 a.m. ready for collection by transport. Each Coy will leave a loading party for this purpose. Rations for tomorrow will also be collected by lorries. Blankets will be tightly rolled in bundles of ten and labelled.

3. All tents and washing bowls now in possession of Coys will be handed in to Q.M. Stores by 5 a.m.

4. One N.C.O. per Coy will proceed on the lorries allotted for stores, as advance party, under 2nd Lieut. SWANSON.

5. Baggage wagons should be used for Officers' kits etc. L.G.S. wagons for Lewis guns and ammunition. Remainder of ammunition on lorries.

6. Full advantage will be taken of the cover from view afforded by hedges and trees when pitching camps. Tents and shelters must be coloured. If [illegible] is not obtainable, mud is to be used.

7. O.'s C. Coys will hand to the Adjutant at the assembly point a certificate that billets have been left clean, and that no Government property has been left behind. Special attention to be paid to Coy. Officers' messes.

8. Billeting returns to be rendered to the Quartermaster by 6·30 a.m.

(Signed). I. M. Sanderson
Capt. and Adjt
15th Garr. Battalion. K.O.Y.L.I.

Copies to all recipients of Order No. 2.

To/ Headquarters,
120th Infantry Brigade. VII A

Weekly Report on Training.

Musketry. With the issue of dummy ammunition and the occasional use of a rifle range, a fair amount of progress has been made in this branch, and more advanced training has been begun.

Lewis Gun. The Lewis Gun teams have devoted almost the whole of their time to this subject, and progress under the Corps School Instructors has been considerable. Most of the men have now fired the gun on the range.

Signalling. 27 men are attending various courses outside the regiment.

Physical Training. The standard of fitness and smartness has improved. Bayonet fighting will shortly begin.

Gas. This branch of training has received a good deal of attention, and a fair stage of efficiency has been reached.

Regimental Courses. The following have been carried out:-

10 N.C.O's in P.T., with occasional supervision by Brigade Instructor;

8 N.C.O's in Musketry (this course has just been started);

8 N.C.O's in Gas Defence;

40 N.C.O's in Handling of Arms and Company Drill (1 hour daily);

8 men in Scouts' Course (the need of a Scout Officer and Scout Sergeant is noticeable).

Route Marching. Marching without packs is up to the standard required.

Lt.-Col.
Commanding
15th Bn., K.O.Y.L.I.

SECRET. VII Copy No. 3.

15th Battalion King's Own Yorkshire Light Infantry. Order No 3

Ry Maps 26.6.1918
36a N.W.
36a N.E.
1/20000

1. 15th Battalion K.O.Y.L.I. Order No 1 is cancelled and the following substituted.

2. In the event of an enemy attack on the Second Army front, the 120th Brigade, and attached troops, will man the W. HAZEBROUCK Line from D 26 c 4.3 to C 6 d 8.2.

3. The 15th K.O.Y.L.I., with attached troops, will man the central sub-section of this line.
Boundaries of Battalion sub-section are as follows:-
Southern Boundary from D 19 a 3.2 (road exclusive) - along road to C 24 a 9.4 - Cross roads C 23 b 2.3
Northern Boundary D 7 c 5.2 - C 18 b 8.8 - C 11 c 9.1.

4. The following from 26th Labour Group will be attached to the Battalion

UNIT	STRENGTH
84th Labour Coy.	364 rifles
92nd Labour Coy.	372 "
110th Labour Coy.	332 "

The above will report on alarm to 2nd Lieut. H.E. TAYLOR, and 3 guides to be detailed by R.S.M., at X roads C 14 d 2.5

5. The Battalion sector will be held as follows:-
Right Outpost Coy. - "R" Coy from D 19 a 3.2 to D 13 d 3.7 (road inclusive)
Left Outpost Coy. - "Q" Coy from D 13 d 3.7 (road exclusive) to D 7 c 5.2.
Each Outpost Coy will have three platoons in the front line, and one in close support, and will have listening posts in front of the Main Line of Resistance.
Right Support Coy. - "T" Coy. C 24 b 9.3 to C 18 d 9.6
Left Support Coy. - "S" Coy C 18 d 9.6 to C 12 b 0.7.
The Support Coys will be organised in depth.
Reserve - Labour Coys as detailed in Para 4.
C 24 b 0.4 - C 12 b 4.1
Battalion Headquarters will be at C 18 c 3.9.
Regimental Aid Post near Battalion Headquarters.

6. Commanders of Outpost Coys are responsible for liaison with Coys on their respective flanks.

7. It must be impressed on all ranks that they are to hold the line in which they are posted, whether it be the Observation or Main Line, to the last man.

No withdrawal of troops will take place, even from the Line of Observation, unless orders to that effect are received from Battalion Headquarters.

8. The following will be carried to the trenches:-

120 rounds S.A.A. on each man
2000 rounds " per Lewis gun

1 day's rations and 1 day's iron ration } on each man.

9. Coy Commanders will prepare a scheme for the defence of their sector, and will forward copies to Battalion Headquarters as soon as possible.

10. Instructions in regard to action to be taken are the same as those issued separately in connection with Order No 1

11. On receipt of orders to move, all Lewis guns and filled magazines will be dumped in transport lines at once, and also the 23 filled petrol tins in possession of Coys. and the 8 in possession of Battalion Headquarters.

A Battalion Dump will be formed near X roads at C 17 d 9.1, where Lewis Guns, S.A.A. and petrol tins will be dumped.

12. In the event of the Battalion becoming engaged, Headquarters will move forward. The exact ~~position~~ location will be notified later to all concerned.

(Signed) L M Sandison Capt & Adjt
15th Battn, K.O.Y.L.I.

Copy No	1	C.O.
"	2	Adjutant
"	3	War Diary
"	4	File
"	5	Q Coy
"	6	R "
"	7	S "
"	8	T "
"	9	Quartermaster
"	10	Medical Officer
"	11	Transport Officer
"	12	R.S.M.
"	13	120th Infantry Brigade
"	14	26th Labour Group

Instructions regarding War Diaries and Intelligence Summaries are contained in F. S. Regs., Part II. and the Staff Manual respectively. Title pages will be prepared in manuscript.

WAR DIARY or ~~INTELLIGENCE SUMMARY.~~

(Erase heading not required.)

Page 1. July 1918 VOL. II

Army Form C. 2118.

15th K.O.Y.L.I

15TH BATTN. K.O.Y.L.I. No. 15/53H Date 2-8-18

40/120

2

Place	Date	Hour	Summary of Events and Information	Remarks and references to Appendices
LA BELLE HOTESSE	1/7/18		Training. Weather still continues, dry, warm, & bright. Water getting low.	JRB
do. do.	2/7/18		The 120th Brigade was inspected by H.R.H. The DUKE OF CONNAUGHT – BRIG. GEN. HOBKIRK in command of the Brigade – Opened regimental canteen for the men.	JRB
do. do.	3/7/18		Lieut. Col. F.C. McCordick left the Bn. to proceed to CANADA for duty with his own unit there. Lieut. Col. T.W.T. ISAAC, assumed command from this date.	JRB
do. do.	4/7/18		All men confined to camp owing to epidemic of SPANISH FLU.	JRB
do. do.	5/7/18		Training continued. The M.O. Capt. C.H. CARROLL left to take charge of a C.C.S. his successor Capt. J.M. RYAN, arrived.	JRB
do. do.	6/7/18		The C.O. & ADJ. visited Bn. sector of W. HAZEBROUCK line. Bn. transport inspected by BRIG. GEN. HOBKIRK. He ~~complimented~~ expressed himself satisfied with ~~the~~ T.O. on the condition of the horses & vehicles.	JRB

A6945 Wt. W11422/M1160 350,000 12/16 D. D. & L. Forms/C./2118/14.

Instructions regarding War Diaries and Intelligence Summaries are contained in F. S. Regs., Part II. and the Staff Manual respectively. Title pages will be prepared in manuscript.

Page 2.

WAR DIARY
or
~~INTELLIGENCE SUMMARY.~~
(Erase heading not required.)

July 1918

VOL. II

Army Form C. 2118.

15th K.O.Y.L.I.

Place	Date	Hour	Summary of Events and Information	Remarks and references to Appendices
LA BELLE HOTESSE	7/7/18		Bn. church parade conducted by Bn. PADRE, CAMPBELL-DOUGLAS. JRB	
do. do.	8/7/18		Training. Weather changing, thunder & some sharp bursts of rain. JRB	
do. do.	9/7/18		Bn. inspected at work, in the afternoon by G.O.C 40th DIV. MAJ. GEN. PATON. A highly satisfactory report was afterwards received by the C.O. JRB	Appendix I
LE ROMARIN	10/7/18		The Bn. occupied their sector of the W. HAZEBROUCK Line. MAJ. GEN. PATON G.O.C. 40th DIV. & BRIG. GEN. HOBKIRK inspected the line. Weather unsettled. JRB	
	11/7/18 12/7/18 13/7/18		Bn. in W. HAZEBROUCK Line JRB	Appendix II
	14/7/18		Returned to Quarters at LA BELLE HOTESSE JRB	

A6945 Wt. W11422/M1160 350,000 12/16 D. D. & L. Forms/C./2118/14.

Instructions regarding War Diaries and Intelligence Summaries are contained in F. S. Regs., Par. II. and the Staff Manual respectively. Title pages will be prepared in manuscript.

Page 3.

WAR DIARY
or
~~INTELLIGENCE SUMMARY.~~
(Erase heading not required.)

July 1918

VOL. II

Army Form C. 2118.

15th K.O.Y.L.I.

Place	Date	Hour	Summary of Events and Information	Remarks and references to Appendices
LA BELLE HOTESSE	15/7/18		Cleaning up + Training. Forenoons now to be devoted to intensive training, Afternoons to Sports + games JKB	
			Violent thunder storm at 5 AM torrential rain	
do. do	16/7/18		Training. Selected Bn Football team JKB	
do. do	17/7/18		Training. Conference of Bn. Commanders + O/C Coys. with G.O.C. DIV. at WALLEN CAPPEL. This took the form of an address by the G.O.C. JKB	
do. do	18/7/18		Training. Bn drill under 2nd in Command. Played the 11th CAMERON HIGHRS at football, beat them by 1 goal to NIL. JKB	
do. do	19/7/18		On range + baths. PLAYED the 10th K.O.S.B.s at football beat them by 2 goals to 1.	
do. do	20/7/18		Training. Good news about the FRENCH at SOISSONS having captured 21000 HUNS + 400 GUNS	
do. do	21/7/18		The 40th DIV. attended DIVINE SERVICE, + thereafter marched passed the G.O.C. MAJ. GEN. PATON in column of route.	

A6945 Wt. W11422/M1160 350,000 12/16 D. D. & L. Forms/C./2118/14.

Instructions regarding War Diaries and Intelligence Summaries are contained in F. S. Regs., Part II. and the Staff Manual respectively. Title pages will be prepared in manuscript.

Page 4.

WAR DIARY
or
~~INTELLIGENCE SUMMARY.~~
(Erase heading not required.)

July 1918
VOL. II

Army Form C. 2118.

15th K.O.Y.L.I.

Place	Date	Hour	Summary of Events and Information	Remarks and references to Appendices
LA BELLE HOTESSE	22/7/18		Orders received that Brigade will now defend the EAST HAZEBROUCK line. C.O. & officers reconnoitred Bn sector of this line	JRB
do. do.	23/7/18		Heavy rain all day – training had to be abandoned –	JRB
do. do.	24/7/18		Training, open warfare	JRB
do. do.	25/7/18		Training, Range etc. Officers riding school started.	JRB
do. do.	26/7/18		Training. Weather very broken, high wind.	JRB
do. do.	27/7/18		Heavy rain, training suspended till noon. Played the	JRB
do. do.	"		17th Bn. Worcester Regiment at football, beat them 3 goals to 1.	JRB
do. do.	28/7/18		Divine service conducted by Chaplain Campbell. Douglas. Short ceremonial drill thereafter. 4 Field Cookers arrived	JRB
do. do.	29/7/18		Working parties called for by Brigade. Remainder of Bn continued training. Weather changed to, Fine & Warm	JRB
do. do.	30/7/18		Bn. inspected at work by MAJ. Gen. PATON.	JRB

Instructions regarding War Diaries and Intelligence Summaries are contained in F. S. Regs., Part II, and the Staff Manual respectively. Title pages will be prepared in manuscript.

Page 5.

WAR DIARY
~~or~~
~~INTELLIGENCE SUMMARY.~~
(*Erase heading not required.*)

July 1918
VOL. II

Army Form C. 2118.

15th B.O.Y.L.I.

Place	Date	Hour	Summary of Events and Information	Remarks and references to Appendices
LA BELLE HOTESSE	31/7/18		Training – Advance party left for LUMBRES. Bn follows on 2nd Aug. to undergo 4 days intensive musketry training. Played the 10th K.O.S.B. at Football, return match, the K.O.S.B. beat us by 5 goals to 2.	Appendix III.
			2-8-18. T.W.T. [illegible] Lt.-Col. Comdg 15th Bn KOYLI.	

A6945 Wt. W11422/M1160 350,000 12/16 D. D. & L. Forms/C./2118/14.

— COPY —

Inspection

appendix I War Diary

Report by Maj. Gen. Commdg. 40th Division

120th Inf. Brigade

15th Batt. K O Y L I

" Turn-out very good. Steadiness on parade, handling of arms, and marching very good.

Company and Platoon Commanders commanded and gave instruction personally in quite a satisfactory manner.

Musketry instruction good (I saw no shooting)

Lewis Gun training the best I have seen so far.

Camp clean and tidy.

Canteen accommodation good but a poor stock. More interest shewn in it than elsewhere.

Regimental Transport very good. Horses well groomed and in good condition."

SECRET II COPY NO. 2

15th Battalion Kings Own Yorkshire Light Infantry

Para 5 of 15th K.O.Y.L.I. Order No 3 as amended by "Amendment to Order No 3" is cancelled, and the following substituted:-

5. Coys in the front system will occupy the MAIN LINE of Resistance and part of the Outpost Line with observation posts pushed out in front. The Battalion Sector will be held as follows:-

(a) Right Coy - 'R' from D 19 a 5 2 (road exclusive) to D 13 c 6 3 (gap inclusive)

Centre Coy - 'S' from D 13 c 6.3 (gap exclusive) to D 13 b 2 2 (road inclusive)

Left Coy - 'Q' from D 13 b 2.2 (road exclusive) to D 7 c 6 3

Each Coy will have 3 platoons in the MAIN LINE and one platoon in the Outpost Line, and will have an observation post not less than 300 yards in front of the Outpost Line

(b) Right Support Coy - "T" - from C 24 b 9 3 to C 18 d 8.6 with one platoon in rear

Left Support Coy - 35th Labour Coy from C 18 d 8.6 to C 18 a 9.6

(c) Right Reserve Coy - 31st Labour Coy from C 24 b 0.4 to C 18 c 7.5

Left Reserve Coy - 92nd Labour Coy from C 18 c 7.5 to C 12 c 4.0

NOTE The MAIN LINE of Resistance is the line which is heavily wired and marked with boards 'FRONT LINE'

(d) Battalion H.Qrs at C 18 c 3 9

Regimental Aid Post near Battalion H.Qrs

(sgd) J. W. Swanson
2nd Lieut & A/Adjt
15th Battalion K.O.Y.L.I

COPIES TO:-

1 C.O
2 War Diary
3 File
4-7 Q.R.S.T. Coys
8. Q.M
9 T.O
10 M.O.
11 31st Labour Coy
12 92nd Labour Coy
13 35th Labour Coy
14 120th Infantry Brigade

11-7-18

Appendix III

Copy No. 3

SECRET

15th Battalion King's Own Yorkshire Light Infantry.

ORDER NO. 6

1-8-1918.

Map
HAZEBROUCK 5A
Sheet 36A.

1. The Battalion, less Details, will move to LUMBRES tomorrow entraining at WARDRECQUES Station at 4-30 pm

2. The Battalion will assemble at the Cross Roads C.14.d. 20.45. ready to move off at 1-30 pm
Dress: Marching Order less blankets & packs.
Steel helmets will be carried.
Order of march - B. C. D. A. Coys, Headquarters.

3 2nd Lieut G.W.W. DRON will act as entraining Officer and report to R.T.O. WARDRECQUES Station at 3-15 pm

4 The whole of the first-line Transport including ammunition will move by road to LUMBRES, without staging.
Time of Starting:- 1-30 pm

(Signed) L.M. Sandison Capt & Adjt
15th Battalion, K.O.Y.L.I.

Copy No. 1 .. C.O.
2 Adjutant
3 .. War Diary
4 File
5 .. A Coy
6 B "
7 C "
8 D
9 Quartermaster
10 Medical Officer
11 Transport Officer
12 .. R.S.M.

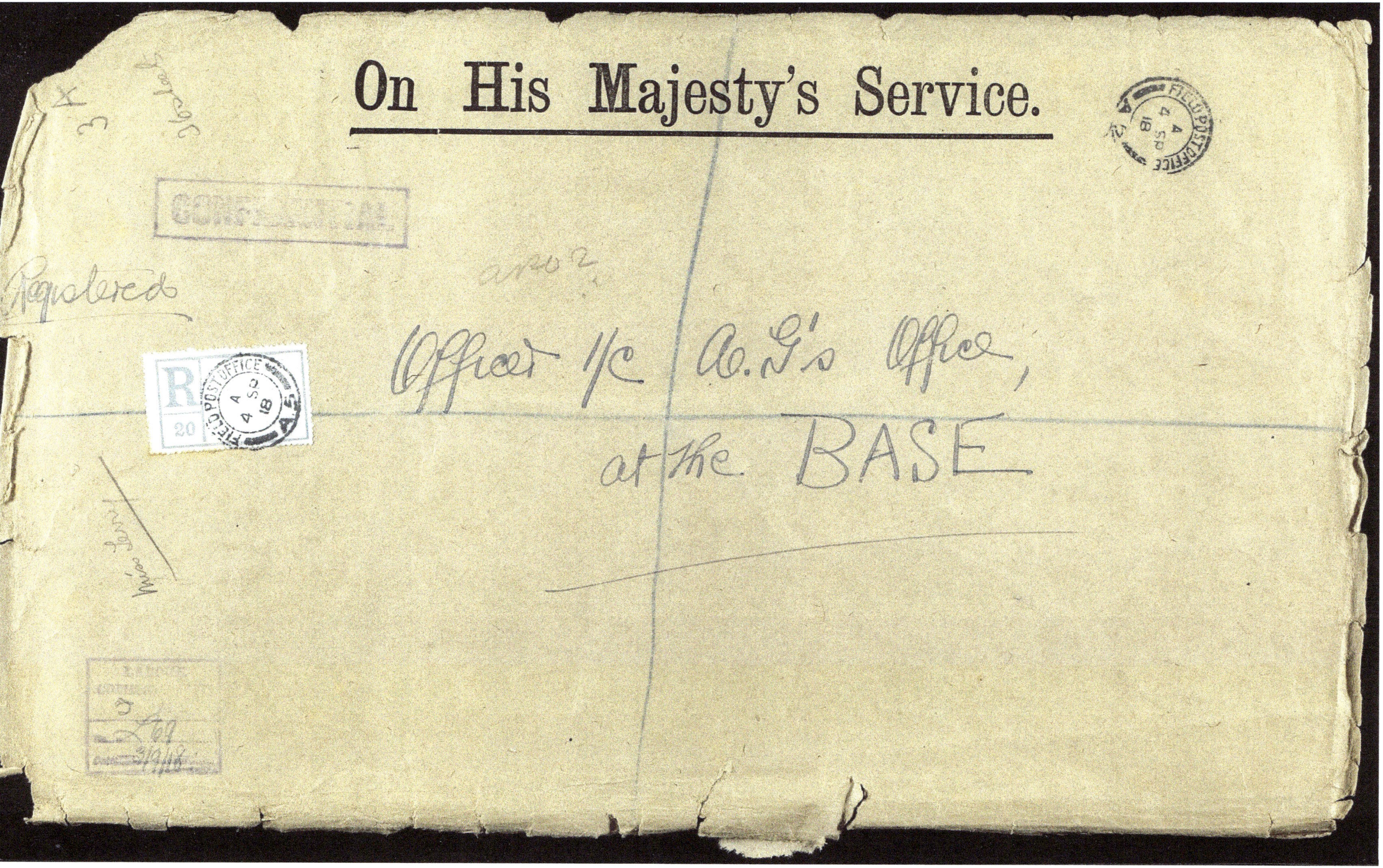
On His Majesty's Service.
FIELD POST OFFICE 4 SP 18
CONFIDENTIAL
Registered
R 20
Officer i/c A.G's Office,
at the BASE

15th Battalion

King's Own Yorkshire Light Infantry

WAR DIARY

1st - 31st August, 1918

Vol No. III August. 1918. 15th Battalion R.O.Y.L.I. Army Form C. 2118.

Instructions regarding War Diaries and Intelligence Summaries are contained in F. S. Regs., Part II. and the Staff Manual respectively. Title pages will be prepared in manuscript.

WAR DIARY
or
INTELLIGENCE SUMMARY.
(*Erase heading not required.*)

Place	Date	Hour	Summary of Events and Information	Remarks and references to Appendices
LA. BELLE HOTESSE	1/8/18		Lieut. Col. BLACK. GSO 40th DIV. inspected Bn. when training Officers fired revolver course.	
do. do.	2/8/18		Left LA BELLE HOTESSE at 1-30 p.m. for LUMBRES. Marched to WARDRECQUES, entrained there, after waiting on train from 3-30 p.m. till 6 p.m. - Arrived LUMBRES 7-30 p.m. marched to Camp about 3 Kilometers. Men under canvas. Officers billeted in large Chateau standing in spacious grounds. Bn. mess established for first time. Heavy rain throughout the day	APPENDIX No. 1
LUMBRES	3/8/18		Intensive training on range all day.	
do.	4/8/18		Range all day. Lieut. Col. T.W.T. ISAAC attended a service in the LUMBRES CHURCH on the occasion of the 4th anniversary of the WAR	
do.	5/8/18		At the Range. Weather unsettled, making shooting difficult 3 new Officers arrived all 2nd Lieuts.	

A6945 Wt. W11422/M1160 350,000 12/16 D. D. & L. Forms/C./2118/14.

2.

Vol. No III   August, 1918   15th Battalion K.O.Y.L.I.

Instructions regarding War Diaries and Intelligence Summaries are contained in F. S. Regs., Part II. and the Staff Manual respectively. Title pages will be prepared in manuscript.

WAR DIARY
or
~~INTELLIGENCE SUMMARY.~~
(Erase heading not required.)

Army Form C. 2118.

Place	Date	Hour	Summary of Events and Information	Remarks and references to Appendices
LUMBRES	6/8/18		Field firing on range. Thereafter all Coys competed in the ARA Platoon competition. D Coy was first & received the Prize subscribed by the Bn Officers of Frs 54. Area Commandant Full Colonel & Officer i/c Range dined with the Officers	
do	7/8/18		Left LUMBRES by Motor Lorries at 12-30 pm arrived back at LA BELLE HOTESSE 4 p.m.	No 2.
LA BELLE HOTESSE	8/8/18		Training & innoculation. Lecture to Bn by Acting Brigadier Lieut Col ARCHER-SHEE D.S.O. M.P. on the "Effect of British Sea Power Supremacy on the WAR"	
do	9/8/18		Training	
do	10/8/18		Training.	
do	11/8/18		Left LA BELLE HOTESSE for LE TIR ANGLAIS relieving the 23rd LANCASHIRE FUSILIERS in reserve to the 121st BRIGADE	No 2A.
LE TIR ANGLAIS	12/8/18		Moved from LE TIR ANGLAIS to Support position in AVAL WOOD (See Appendix) relieving the 10th EAST YORKS	No 3

A6945 Wt. W11422/M1160 350,000 12/16 D. D. & L. Forms/C./2118/14.

Vol. No III. August, 1918. 15th Battalion, K.O.Y.L.I.

WAR DIARY
or
INTELLIGENCE SUMMARY.
(Erase heading not required.)

Army Form C. 2118.

Instructions regarding War Diaries and Intelligence Summaries are contained in F. S. Regs., Part II. and the Staff Manual respectively. Title pages will be prepared in manuscript.

Place	Date	Hour	Summary of Events and Information	Remarks and references to Appendices
LE TIR ANGLAIS	12/8/18		and being attached to the 92nd BRIGADE. Weather, fine dry & warm. Lieut. WALTERS slightly gassed (MUSTARD) while superintending a working Party.	
AVAL WOOD	13/8/18		The Bn. relieved the 11th EAST LANCS (3 Coys) & the 11th EAST YORKS (one coy) in Front Line. One Coy. 11th E. YORKS relieved the the RIGHT FRONT Coy. Sector held by the 11th EAST LANCS & are under orders of the O.C. 15th KOYLI. During the relief One Sergt. was Killed & 10 O/R wounded.	No. 4. No. 5.
FRONT LINE	14/8/18		Holding the Line. Lewis Gun Team of 2 Corpls & 2 Ptes killed by Hun T.M.	
do	15/8/18		Holding the Line. One Coy. of 11th E. YORKS on our left advanced about 500 yds sustaining severe casualties. Left Platoon of B. Coy 15 KOYLI moved also forward & kept in touch, no casualties during this advance. Casualties during the day 5 O/R wounded	

4.

Vol. No. III.   August, 1918.   15th Battalion K.O.Y.L.I.

Army Form C. 2118.

Instructions regarding War Diaries and Intelligence Summaries are contained in F. S. Regs., Part II. and the Staff Manual respectively. Title pages will be prepared in manuscript.

WAR DIARY
or
~~INTELLIGENCE SUMMARY.~~
(Erase heading not required.)

Place	Date	Hour	Summary of Events and Information	Remarks and references to Appendices
FRONT LINE	16/8/18		Holding the Line. Heavily bombarded at intervals throughout the day by HUN T M & Heavies. Casualties throughout the day 5 O/R wounded	
do	17/8/18		Relieved by 11th CAMERONS at 10 p m. Previous to relief at about 8-30 p m HUN bombarded whole line with T M. Casualties 5 O/R wounded. Marched back to LE TIR ANGLAIS in reserve. Total Casualties during tour in Front Line 1 Sergt. 2 Corpls. 2 Privates KILLED 25 O/R WOUNDED	No. 6. No. 7.
LE TIR ANGLAIS	18/8/18		Cleaning up. Working party of 75 supplied at night. Message received from G.O.C. 40th DIV. thanking the Bn for their good work & steadiness in the Front Line. This was read out to the Bn. in the evening	
do.	19/8/18		WORKING PARTIES. 40th DIV. HORSE SHOW held at RENESCURE. C.O. & ADJ. attended.	

5. Vol. No. III. August, 1918. 15th Battalion, K.O.Y.L.I.

Instructions regarding War Diaries and Intelligence Summaries are contained in F. S. Regs., Part II. and the Staff Manual respectively. Title pages will be prepared in manuscript.

WAR DIARY
or
INTELLIGENCE SUMMARY.
(Erase heading not required.)

Army Form C. 2118.

Place	Date	Hour	Summary of Events and Information	Remarks and references to Appendices
LE TIR ANGLAIS	20/8/18		Bn moved into Brigade Support. Bn head H. Qrs at AVAL WOOD – 2 Coys in "Z" Line – 2 Coys in neighbourhood of Bn. head H Qrs	
AVAL WOOD	21/8/18		Working Parties	
do	22/8/18		Bn moved to forward Zone – 2 coys in Front Line (PONT RODIN to COCHIN CORNER.)	No. 8.
			2 Coys. in support in preparation for attack tomorrow	No. 9.
do	23/8/18		Bn attacked on a line from PONT RODIN – COCHIN CORNER — 1st OBJECTIVE LAUDICK BECQUE	
			2nd do. BECKET, CORNER – BISHOPS. CORNER. RD	No. 10 + 11.
do	24/8/18		Holding Line Active patrolling	
do	25/8/18		No active operations engaged in. Consolidating	No. 12.
			positions already gained	No. 13.
do	26/8/18		Holding Line	No. 14. / No. 15
do	27/8/18		"C" coy 15th K.O.Y.L.I (Capt GARROD) on the left, + gained	No. 16.
			objective on road PONT RONDIN – BISHOPS CORNER	No. 17

A6945 Wt. W11422/M1160 350,000 12/16 D. D. & L. Forms/C./2118/14.

6.

Vol. No III. August, 1918.

Instructions regarding War Diaries and Intelligence Summaries are contained in F. S. Regs., Part II, and the Staff Manual respectively. Title pages will be prepared in manuscript.

15th Battalion, K.O.Y.L.I.

WAR DIARY or ~~INTELLIGENCE SUMMARY.~~

(Erase heading not required.)

Army Form C. 2118.

Place	Date	Hour	Summary of Events and Information	Remarks and references to Appendices
AVAL WOOD	27/8/18	10AM	During operations 'D' coy captured 5 Prisoners & 'C' Coy 7 Prisoners & one Machine gun brought back. The 2 (TWO) KOYLI Front Coys relieved at night by the 11th Camerons	No 18.
do.				
	28/8/18		Holding line 2 Coys. CAMERONS & B. Coy 15 KOYLI the latter sent out 3 strong Patrols & reported Road BOWERY COTTAGES — RUE PROVOST clear of enemy but in Plantation adjacent to BOWERY COTTAGES machine GUN Post & Snipers Post active	
do	29/8/18		Bn. relieved by 11th CAMERONS & moved back into support.	No 19 No 20. No 21.
do	30/8/18		In support - Moved in afternoon to WALLEN CAPPEL	No 22.
do	31/8/18		Baths & cleaning up	No 23.
				No 24.

J Ralston Bock
Major
15th Bn K.O.Y.L.I.

A6945 Wt. W11422/M1160 350,000 12/16 D. D. & L. Forms/C./2118/14.

Secret Appendix NO 1 Copy No 3

Administrative Instructions

MOVE :- 2ND AUGUST 1918

To accompany 15TH Battalion K.O.Y.L.I. Order No 6

1-8-18

1. The following will be dumped at Quartermaster's Stores by 10 a.m.:-
Blankets (tightly rolled in bundles of 10, and labelled).
Officer's Valises
Any essential Company Stores,
Packs, clearly marked with name and number.
Officer's Mess Boxes will be dumped not later than 1.30 P.M.
Lewis Gun Officer will arrange for all Lewis Guns and equipment to be loaded in Transport Lines by 10. AM.
O.C. "A" Company will detail a loading party of 1 N.C.O. and 15 men to report to Q.M. at 12 noon.

2. Personnel, as detailed separately, will remain behind under 2ND Lieut. THEWLIS.

3. Officers Commanding Companies will hand to the Adjutant at the Assembly Point, marching-out states, and certificates that encamping grounds have been left clean.

4. Baggage Wagons should be used for Officer's Valises etc; L.G.S. Wagons for Lewis Guns and Ammunition.
Lorries will convey packs to WARDREQUES Station, where they will be collected by the men and carried with them in the train.
Lorries will then return for blankets etc, which will be conveyed to LUMBRES.

(Signed) L. M. Sandison, Capt. Adjt
15th Battalion K.O.Y.L.I.

Copy No
1 ... C.O.
2 ... Adjutant
3 ... War Diary
4 ... File
5 ... "A" Co
6 ... "B" Co
7 ... "C" Co
8 ... "D" Co
9 ... Quartermaster
10 ... Medical Officer
11 ... Transport Officer
12 ... R.S.M.

War Diary

Appendix No 2

15th Battalion King's Own Yorkshire Light Infantry.

MOVE 7-8-18

The Battalion will [illegible] in readiness to proceed [illegible] at 12 noon.

Blankets [illegible] will be dumped at the [illegible] by 11.45 am.

Transport will [illegible] at 11-[illegible]

[illegible] under instructions from [illegible].

[illegible] will be [illegible] at the [illegible]

[illegible]

[illegible] 11 am.

[illegible]

Clearing [illegible] to the Adjutant [illegible].

[illegible]
Capt & Adjt.
15th Battn. K.O.Y.L.I.

File

22

SECRET

Appendix no 2A

COPY NO 3

Operation Order NO 7.
by
Lieut Col T W T ISAAC
Commanding 15th Battalion Kings Own Yorkshire Light Infantry

10-8-1918.

Ref. maps.
36A. N.E.
1/20000
36A.
1/40000.

1. The 120th Infantry Brigade will relieve the 121st Infantry Brigade in the Sector West of VIEUX BERQUIN on the night 12/13th instant.

2. The 15th K.O.Y.L.I. will relieve the 23rd Lancs. Fus. in Reserve Area about D 12 a and D 12 C, and D 17 on 11th instant.
Coys. will relieve corresponding Coys. of the 23rd Lancs Fus.

3. The Battalion will parade in column of route in the following order:- C. D. A. B. Headquarters.
Starting Point:- C 14 d 6.2.
Coys. march off at 5 minutes interval. Time 1.0 pm.
3 minutes interval between Platoons East of the MORBECQUE - HAZEBROUCK road.
ROUTE:- MILL - FONTAINE Cross Roads C 16 d 2.3.
C 17 a 9.1 DAKAR COTTAGE.
DRESS:- marching order less packs. S.B.R's at alert.

4. All maps, photographs, defence schemes, trench stores will be taken over from Unit relieved, and receipts forwarded to Battalion Hd. Qrs. as soon as possible after relief.

5. Completion of relief to be reported as already arranged.

6. Marching out states and certificates of cleanliness of Coy. Lines will be handed to Adjutant before marching off.

(sgd) L. M. Henderson
Major; a/Adj
15th Battalion K.O.Y.L.I.

Copy NO 1 - C.O.
" 2 - Adjutant
" 3 - War Diary
" 4 - File
" 5-8 - A-D Coys.
" 9 - Q.M.
" 10 - T.O.
" 11 - M.O.
" 12 - R.S.M.
" 13 - 120th Bde.
" 14 - 23rd Lancs. Fus.

Appendix No 3

SECRET. 15th Battalion K.O.Y.L.I. COPY NO. 3

Relief Order No 1.
by
Lieut. Col. T.W.[illegible] ISAAC
Commanding.

12-7-191[illegible]

REF MAP
36^A N.E.
1/20000.

1. The Battalion will move to the vicinity of E 2[illegible] [illegible], relieving the 10th EAST YORKS, 92nd Bde.

2. The Battalion will move off in the following order:
D. B. A. Battalion H.Q. [illegible]
D. Coy starting at 5.30 p.m. 200 yards interval between platoons.
Dress:- Fighting order.
Starting Point:- D 17 a 7.0.
Route:- PAPOTE - SCALLOP FARM - SWING BRIDGE.
Guides at E 25 a 9.9.
2 Lieut FISHER will guide the Battalion.

3. TRANSPORT. Convoy of Transport under Transport Officer will follow the Battalion:-
   1. [illegible]
   2. Coy [illegible] & H.Q. [illegible]
   3. Baggage Wagon.
   4. [illegible]

4. GREATCOATS will be rolled in bundles of 10 and stacked on the road near Coy. H.Qrs. by 4.30 p.m.
1 N.C.O. and 1 man per Coy. will be detailed as guards over greatcoats.

5. PETROL TINS. The 23 petrol tins for Coys and [illegible] for Battalion H.Qrs. will be [illegible] [illegible] by [illegible].

6. LOCATIONS.

Battalion H.Qrs.	- E 25 a 7.4.
A Company	- E 2[illegible] d.
B	- E 21 b.
C	- E 2[illegible] b.
D	- E 27 [illegible] and E 2[illegible] d.
Transport Lines	- [illegible] 12 b 7.7.
92nd Bde H.Qrs	- D 24 a 9.0.

Sgd [illegible]
Major [illegible]
15th Battalion K.O.Y.L.I.

COPIES TO:-
1. - C.O.
2. - Adjutant
3. - [illegible]
4. - Bde
5. - A Coy
6. - B
7. - C
8. - D
9. - R.S.M.
10. - Q.M.
11. - T.O.
12. - M.O.
13. - Intelligence Officer
14. - Signalling
15. - 120th Bde.

SECRET. 15th Battalion K.O.Y.L.I. Appendix No 4 Copy No 3.

Relief Order No 2.
by
Lieut. Colonel [illegible] Commdg.

13.8.1918

Ref. Map. 36A N.E. 1/20000.

1. The Battalion will be relieved by 11th Camerons today and will relieve 11th E. Lancs (3 Coys) and 11th E. Yorks (1 Coy) in Front Line.

2. Coys will march off independently as follows:
   - 'B' Coy – 10 p.m.
   - 'D' " – 10 p.m.
   - 'A' " – 10 p.m.
   - 'C' " – 10 p.m.

   200 yards between Platoons.
   Order of precedence on road :- D.B.C.A.
   Dress:- Fighting Order.

3. **Relief**

   Front Line.
   Right Coy: 'D' Coy 15th K.O.Y.L.I. relieves Z Coy 11th E. Lancs
   Left Coy: 'B' " " " " Right Front Coy 11th E. Yorks

   Support Line.
   Right Coy: 'C' Coy " " " W Coy 11th E. Lancs
   Left " 'A' " " " " Y " " "

   5. Guides per Coy. will report to Coys as follows:
   - A Coy guides at A Coy Hd Qrs at 10 a.m.
   - B " " " B " " " 10 "
   - C " " " C " " " 9.45 "
   - D " " " D " " " 10 "

   Completion of relief will be wired to Battalion Hd Qrs as already arranged.

4. (a) [illegible]
   (b) Lewis Guns.
   (c) Greatcoats.
   (d) Petrol tins.

   } Separate instructions have been issued to all concerned.

5. **Relief.** Lists of Trench Stores, Maps etc and [illegible] taken over will be sent to Battalion Hd Qrs by 1st Orderly after relief.

6. **Attached Troops.** 1 Coy of 11th E. Yorks will relieve the Right Front Line Coy of 11th E. Lancs and will come under the orders of O.C. 15th K.O.Y.L.I.

7. **Discipline.** No movement of any kind will take place by day.

8. **Locations:-**

Battalion Hd Qrs at	E.27.c.0.9.
R.A.P.	K.4.a.2.0.
Transport Lines	C.12.b.7.7.
A Coy Hd Qrs	E.28.a.2.2.
B " "	—
C " "	K.4.a.4.7.
D " "	K.5.b.5.4.
Bde Hd Qrs	D.24.a.7.1.

(Sgd) C. M. Sanders
Major & Adjt.
15th Bn. K.O.Y.L.I.

9. Acknowledge.

Copies to:
- 1.- C.O.
- 2.- [illegible]
- 3 - War Diary
- 4 - File.
- 5-8 - A-D Coys.
- 9 - R.S.M.
- 10 - Q.M.
- 11.- T.O.
- 12 - M.O.
- 13 - Intelligence Officer
- 14 - Signalling "
- 15 - 120th Brigade
- 16 - 11th E. Yorks
- 17 - 11th E. Lancs.

War Diary

Appendix no 5

15th BATTALION, KING'S OWN YORKSHIRE LIGHT INFANTRY.

ACCOUNT OF OPERATIONS FROM 13TH AUGUST, TO 29TH AUGUST, 1918.

On the nights of the 13th/14th ~~and~~ to 17th/18th, the line was held as follows:-

"D" Company - right out-post Company, from GARS BRUGGE FARM to east of CORNET PERDU.

"B" Company - left outpost Company, east of VERTE RUE.

"A" and "C" Companies in "Z" line.

During this period no operations took place, except that the left of "B" Company was swung forward about 150 yards on the night of 15th/16th August, in order to conform with the advance made by the E. YORKS BATTALION on our left. During this operation Privates WARD and CARTER earned the Military Medal.

The battalion was withdrawn to LE TIR ANGLAIS on the night of the 17th/18th, and moved up into support on the night of the 21st/22nd.

SECRET

Appendix no 6

Copy No. 2

15th Battalion King's Own Yorkshire Light Infantry Order No 3 by Lieut. Colonel T.W.T. Isaac Commanding

16. 8. 1918.

1. The 11th Battalion CAMERON HIGHLANDERS will relieve the 15th Battalion K.O.Y.L.I. in the Forward Zone on the night 17/18th August. On completion of relief the 15th K.O.Y.L.I. will move into Reserve relieving 10th K.O.S.B.

2. A Coy. CAMERONS will relieve D Coy. K.O.Y.L.I. (Right Front Line)
B " " " " B " " " (Left " ")
D " " " " C " " " (Right 'Z' Line)
C " " " " A " " " (Left 'Z' Line)

3. All maps, schemes, etc. will be handed over to 11th CAMERONS as well as all trench stores, petrol tins in trench stores, food containers etc. Receipts will be sent to Battalion Hd. Qrs. tomorrow morning.

4. On relief the Battalion will move to LE TIR ANGLAIS.
Route to be followed :- No. 1 & 2 MULE TRACKS (or BEAULIEU FARM road if desired) to Ride 'B' and 'X' Track - D. 30.b.5.2. - FETTLE FARM - SPOOK COTTAGE.
Qr. Mr. will arrange for allotment of accommodation, and will provide hot tea for the Battalion on arrival.

5. A foot inspection will be held immediately on arrival in quarters.

6. Completion of relief will be wired to Battalion Hd. Qrs. in the usual manner.

7. Transport Officer will arrange for conveyance of greatcoats to the new area.

8. Coy. Commanders will provide covering parties while the relief is in progress. Coys. will also provide patrols, details of which will be issued later.

9. Guides
B & D Coys. 1 guide per platoon and one for Coy. Hd. Qrs. will meet incoming Coys. at 9.45 p.m. at junction of 'A' Ride and Track 3.
A & C Coys. guides as above will report direct to relieving Coy. Hd. Qrs. at 8.45 p.m.

10. Trenches, latrines etc., must be left in a clean and sanitary condition.

11. ACKNOWLEDGE.

Sgd. L. H. Sanderson
Major & Adjt.
15th Battalion K.O.Y.L.I.

No 11. to 120 Bde.

Copy No. 1 to C.O.
" " 2 " War Diary
" " 3 " A Coy.
" " 4 " B "
" " 5 " C "
" " 6 " D "
" " 7 " QM and T.O.
" " 8 " M.O.
" " 9 " R.S.M.
" " 10 " 11th CAMERONS

War Diary

File

O.C.

SECRET.

1. RATIONS. 'A' and 'C' Coys. will carry for 'B' and 'D' Coys. as arranged for last night including empty petrol tins.
'C' Coy in addition will provide a party of 1 Sergt and 30 O.R. to carry rations from No 1 Mule Track to 'C' Coy E. Yorks.
Regtl. guides will be at dump at 10 p.m.

2. BURIAL. 'A' Coy. will send 8 men with two stretchers to 'B' Coy to carry bodies to Cemetery.

3. SALVAGE. No salvage returns have yet been received here.

4. HURDLES. It has been noticed on 'Z' line that men have been damaging hurdles by climbing over them. This must cease, and ways may be cut where absolutely necessary.

5. PATROLS. Patrols (Nos decided by Coy. Commdrs) will go out as follows.
'C' Coy. E. Yorks – 1 a.m. to 3 a.m.
Repeat patrol of last night on K.b.c. concerning which no report has been made.
'D' Coy. K.O.Y.L.I. – 10.30 p.m. – 12.30 a.m.
Reconnoitre NO MANS LAND from K.b.c. central to K.b.a. 4.9.
'B' Coy. K.O.Y.L.I. – 1 a.m. to 3 a.m.
Reconnoitre ground in front of advanced posts on left flank (or as desired by Coy. Commdr.)
Full reports should be rendered and any hostile patrols encountered should be engaged, as identification is specially required.
Daylight patrols should also go out when possible to confirm reports.
Boundaries of Company sectors to be adhered to.

16.8.1918.

(Sgd.) L M Sandison
Major and Adjt.
15th Battalion K.O.Y.L.I.

Appendix No 7

SECRET. COPY NO.

Battalion in forward zone and Z line.

15th Battalion K.O.Y.L.I.

DEFENCE ORDERS.

16-8-1918.

1. The Battalion in the forward zone will have two of its own Companies and one Company attached to it from the 92nd Brigade in the forward zone. The attached Company will always be on the right. Its other two companies will garrison the "Z" line. In addition, one Company of the Support Battalion will garrison the Northern portion of the "Z" line and will be under the tactical control of the C.O. of the Battalion holding the forward Zone and "Z" Line.

2. Boundaries of the forward zone and "Z" line are as follows:-

Northern Boundary E 30 central - E 29 central - VOLLEY FARM (exclusive)

Southern Boundary K.11 b 7.4 - K 4 a 6.0.

Boundaries of Companies:-

Forward zone. - K 6 c 4.6 and E 30 c 0.0.
"Z" Line - E 28 c 6.0 and E 28 a 5.0.
Battalion H.Q. at - E 26 b 5.4.
R.A.P. at - K 4 a 2.0.

3. Liaison Posts.

K. 11 b 7.6. (Forward zone)
K 4 c 6.9. ("Z" Line)

4. Action in Case of Attack. There are 3 kinds of warning signals:-

(1) S.O.S.
(2) Gas.
(3) Percy.

Instructions regarding these are issued in appendices I - III.

II. Gas.

Special precautions against gas shelling are to be taken in this Sector, as it is particularly likely to occur in the BOIS D'AVAL area. Steps will be taken to thin out the troops in the gassed area as far as it is possible, and to arrange for their periodical relief.
Our guns will not open fire if no hostile attack is suspected, except at the request of the Infantry.

III. Percy.

If a hostile attack on our front seems to be impending, the code word "PERCY" will be sent.
No reinforcements will be sent, nor counter-attacks made in front of the "Z" line, which will be held at all costs.

Action in the Event of Surprise Attack before "Percy" is Issued.
Troops in the forward zone will hold out at all costs, but will not be reinforced.
The "Z" line will be reinforced as soon as possible as for "Percy", but no counter attack will be made in front of the "Z" line until the force of the enemy's attack has been broken.

5. Working Parties. Working parties will always move to their work fully equipped for fighting. In case of heavy bombardment or hostile action indicating an attack, working parties will at once man the nearest defences, reporting to the nearest Unit (Company or Battalion H.Qs) that they have done so, and notifying Battalion H.Qrs. at once.

6. Liaison Between Coys. Coy Commanders will arrange between themselves that patrols between their flank posts go out every half hour during the night at the clock hour and half past the hour, e.g. one Coy. patrol leads at 10 pm, and the other at 10.30 pm.

(Sgd) L. M. Handison
Major & A/Adj.
15th Battalion K.O.Y.L.I.

COPIES TO:-

1. - A Coy.
2. - B "
3. - C "
4. - D "
5. - H. Qrs.
(Copies 1 to 5: To be handed over on relief.)
6. - 120th Brigade

Appendix No 8

COPY NO. 2

SECRET

15th Battalion Kings Own Yorkshire Light Infantry

Order No 7

by

Lieut-Colonel T.W.T. ISAAC

22-8-1918

1. The 15th K.O.Y.L.I. will relieve the 11th Bn Camerons in the forward zone and Z line tonight.
2. C Company K.O.Y.L.I. will relieve D Company Camerons - Front line
   A " " " " B " " Close support line
   B " " moves into centre Z line
   D " " " " right Z line
3. ROUTE for A & C COMPANIES
   X Track, B ride and No 1 mule track. One guide per platoon, and one for Company H.Qrs will meet Companies on No. 1 mule Track near Forward Command post K.5. a. 7.7.
4. Companies will march off independently as follows:-
   "C" Company 9-0 p.m.
   "A" " 9-15 "
   "B" " } under Company arrangement
   "D" }
   200 yards interval will be maintained between platoons.
5. Receipts for all maps, schemes, etc, as well as for all petrol tins, food containers & other Trench Stores will be sent to Battalion H.Qrs. before dawn.
6. Completion of relief will be wired to Bn. H.Qrs in the usual manner.
7. The closest liaison must be maintained both between Companies & platoons & with Companies on either flank, special attention being paid to the right flank (183rd Inf Bde)
8. Os. C. Companies will forward disposition sketches to H.Qrs. before dawn tomorrow.
9. ACKNOWLEDGE

(Sgd) L.M. Sandison
Major & a/adjt
15th Battalion K.O.Y.L.I.

COPIES TO:-

1 - C.O.
2 - War Diary
3 - File
4 - A Company
5 - B "
6 - C "
7 - D "
8 - 11th Camerons
9 - 120th Inf Bde
10 - R.S.M.
11 - T.O.
12 - Q.M.
13 - M.O.

War Diary

 Appendices no 9

On the night of the 22nd/23rd the Battalion relieved the 11TH BATTALION, CAMERON HIGHLANDERS in the Forward Zone. The dispositions were as follows:-

"A" Company - Right Outpost Company, between COCHIN CORNER and GENET CORNER.

"C" Company - Left Outpost Company, between GENET CORNER and PONT RONDIN -

both Companies being west of the VIEUX and and NEUVE BERQUIN ROAD.

"B" and "D" Companies garrisoned the "Z" line.

At 4 p.m. on the 23rd, "A" and "C" Companies attacked the enemy positions. The advance was by means of platoons in artillery formation, preceded by strong fighting patrols. Troops of the 183rd Brigade on our right were believed to be advancing at the same time. As soon as we moved forward a hostile barrage was put down on the road between PONT RONDIN and COCHIN CORNER, and two or three casualties were sustained. The barrage, however, was not very strong, and did not hold up the advance appreciably. Heavy machine gun fire was met with, but Stokes Mortars were of assistance in dealing with this.

"C" Company, on the left, under CAPT. W.R. GARROD, succeeded in advancing about 700 yards, and captured some prisoners. During the operation 2/LIEUT. S.SCARR, with his runner, succeeded in capturing an enemy machine gun, killing or capturing its crew.

On the right the advance of "A" Company, under 2/LIEUT. E. O. DENHAM, was held up for some time, as the troops on our right did not move forward. Eventually the right of this Company moved forward about 50 yards across the road, while the left advanced in touch with "C" Company.

At the close of the day's operations the line ran as fmfollows:-

"A" Company - From COCHIN CORNER to just south of DENVER.

"C" Company - From t at point to L.1.b.8.4.

During the advance the enemy showed considerable enterprise and initiative. He had isolated machine guns and snipers pushed well in advance of his outpost line, and he did not wait to be attacked, but came out into "No-man's-land", and endeavoured to outflank our advancing patrols. He was frequentl- heard to shout what were presumably uncomplimentary remarks.

Appendix 10

CONFIDENTIAL.

120TH INFANTRY BRIGADE INTELLIGENCE SUMMARY
RIGHT SECTOR

6 a.m. 24:8:18 to 6 a.m. 25:8:18.

A. OUR OPERATIONS.

(i) Infantry. Posts established yesterday were further consolidated.

(ii) Patrols. (a) 2/Lieut. J. Parker (15th K.O.Y.L.I) and 6 men proceeded from our posts at L.1.b.6.4. and L.1.b. 7.2. at 8 p.m. to reconnoitre the LAUDICK from L.1.b.7.4. to L.1.d.95.60. The patrol left the above-mentioned posts, proceeded to the LAUDICK at L.1.b.7.4., along the bed of the stream (which is practically dry) to L.1.d.9.6. The patrol observed single shots fired from approx. L.1.b.9.5., apparently a sniper. Enemy M.G. fired at intermediate intervals from approx. L.2.c.5.5. (judging by report). It is presumed that the sniper comes up at dusk, as there was no sniping during the day, 2/Lieut. J. Parker having investigated that portion of the LAUDICK between 4.30 p.m. and 6 p.m. the same day. The patrol returned at 9.30 p.m. by the same route.

(b) Another patrol consisting of 2/Lieut. S. Scarr (15th K.O.Y.L.I.) and 2 men left their post at L.1.d.6.1. at 8 p.m. to reconnoitre ground up to the LAUDICK. The patrol proceeded 50 yds. N. of road running from GENET CORNER to BISHOP'S CORNER and parallel with same until they reached point L.1.d.9.2. They found the enemy holds a post at L.2.c.2.1. where the LAUDICK crosses the road. Post was located by hearing the occupants talking. M.G. postwas located about L.2.c.4.6. by sound and direction of fire.
M.G. post was also located by sound and direction of fire at L.8.a.2.6., position was later confirmed by observing 5 enemy stood upright on the top of the post - 3 of these men were shot by patrol, enemy stretcher bearers were afterwards seen (through field glasses) carrying the bodies away. This post is still active. Patrol returned to our lines at 9.15 p.m.

(c) One Sergt. and 3 men (10th K.O.S.B.) left the post at F.25.d.7.6. at 11 p.m. to get in touch with enemy. They proceeded to F.26.c.8.5. when fired on by M.G. from F.26.d.4.6. M.G. & snipers were also located in line of trees running from L.2.b.0.4. to L.2.b.1.8. Otherwise no sign of enemy between BECKET CORNER and L.1.b.9.9.

(d) One Officer and 3 O.R. (10th K.O.S.B.) left their post at L.1.b.5.8. to get in touch with enemy and locate M.G. positions. The patrol went forward to a depth of 300 yds., and heard enemy speaking, just at that moment a M.G. opened fire from approx. L.2.c.4.8. (judging by report and direction of fire). Patrol returned at 1 a.m.

(e) One Officer and 3 O.R. (10th K.O.S.B.) left our position at L.1.d.2.3. to get in touch with enemy and locate M.G. positions, at 1.30 a.m. The patrol proceeded from L.1.d.2.3. to L.1.b.4.3., L.1.b.9.8., L.1.b.9.8. and L.1.b.8.9. and returned to post at 2.30 a.m. No enemy patrols or signs of enemy seen. There is a line of trip wire about 50 yds. in front of our post.

(iii) Artillery. Usual harassing fire.

T.M's. Nil.
M.G's. Normal.

(vi) Aerial. At 3.30 p.m. one of our 'planes shot down an enemy balloon which fell in flames, a second balloon was brought down at 6 p.m.

Usual formations were observed during the period.

B. ENEMY OPERATIONS.

(i) Infantry. Nil.

(ii) Artillery. / Considerable shelling round COBLEY COTTAGE between 6 and 8 p.m., also at 4 a.m.

/ Active

A barrage was put down on N.30.a. and c. from 12 noon to 12.30 p.m.

At about 11.15 p.m., in response to Red Signals fired from point opposite our left company, right battalion, a heavy barrage was put down on the road from NEW CROSS to GREEN ~~XXXX~~ CORNER and L.1.a. and b., about half an hour later this ceased on Green Signals being fired. N.29.a. received about 25 rounds 77 mm. between 8 p.m. and 8.40 p.m.

N.23.b. and N.5. received much attention.

(iii) M.G's. Fairly active. (See Patrols).

(iv) Snipers. Active at night.

(v) T.M's. Nil.

(vi) Gas Shells. At 8.15 p.m. a few gas shells were fired into back areas.

(vii) Aerial. E.A. observed flying westwards at 8 p.m., which was engaged by A.A. fire.

J. C. Barker Capt.
for Brigadier-General,
Commanding 120th Infantry Brigade.

28:8:18.

Appendix no 11

During the 24th August no further operations were undertaken, but active patrolling was done throughout the day. One patrol found five of the enemy standing on the top of a machine gun post. Three of these were shot by the patrol, and later stretcher-bearers were seen to carry the bodies away.

During the night of the 24th/25th "A" Company was relieved by "B" Company, under CAPT. T.L. [illegible] (who had previously taken up a position about CORNET PERDU, and "D" Company, under CAPT. A. LI[illegible]ERE, relieved "C" Company.

Appendix no 12 Copy no. 3

SECRET.

15th Battalion Kings Own Yorkshire Light Infantry.

Order NO. 8

by

Lieut. Col. T. W. T. ISAAC, Commanding.

2[illegible]-8-1918

1. Companies will relieve each other tonight as follows:-
B Company will relieve A Company in Right Outpost line.
D " " " C " " Left " "
On relief "C" Company will move into dugouts at CORNET PERDU, and "A" Company into the "Z" line (Central Section).

2. B and D Companies will move off as soon as possible after issue of rations, which will be [illegible] after the [illegible], as well as [illegible] [illegible] and [illegible] Tins.

3. Completion of relief will be reported to Battalion H.Qrs in the usual manner.

4. Rations for "A" Company should be taken to "Z" line dump, and issued on arrival of the Company.
Rations for "C" Company will be carried to CORNET PERDU.

Sgd. [illegible] Sanderson,
Major & Adjutant
15th Battalion KOY LI.

COPIES TO :-

1 - C.O.
2 - Adjutant
3 - War Diary
4 - File
5 - A Co
6 - B
7 - C
8 - D
9 - R.S.M.
10 - T.O.
11 - Q.M.
12 - M.O.
13 - 120th Inf Bde

War Diary

Appendix No 14

Secret — Copy No 3

15th Battalion Kings Own Yorkshire Light Infantry

Order No 9

by

Lieut Col. T. W. T. Isaac. Commanding

26. 8. 19

1. The following inter-company Reliefs will be carried out on the night of the 26th/27th August 1918.
   C. Company will relieve 'D' Company in left Outpost Line.
   On being relieved D Company will relieve 'B' Company in Right Outpost Line.
   On being relieved 'B' Company will move into support at CORNET PERDU.

2. 'C' Company will draw their own rations and water from Ration Dump at 9-30 P.M. These will be issued and carried forward on the men as well as Lewis Guns and Magazines. Rations for 'D' Company will be carried to H.Q. Right Outpost Company, arriving there about 12 midnight. On arrival at CORNET PERDU. "B" Company will draw their own rations from Ration Dump

3. O.C. 'D' Company will send the usual 5 guides to C. Company by 9-0 P.m.
   O.C. "B" Company will send guides to "D" Company by 10.10 P.m and will also reconnoitre the position at CORNET PERDU before C. Company move forward.

4. On arrival in right outpost line O.C. 'D' Company will locate as far as possible any enemy machine gun posts in front of his line by means of active patrolling, in order to ensure the effective co-operation of Stokes Mortars during operations on the 27th August.

5. Completion of Relief will be wired to Advanced H.Q. in the usual way

6. Ration Dumps for 'B, C, D' Coys will be to-night near road junction K11. b. 5.8.

7. Acknowledge

(Signed) L. M. Sandison
Major and Adjutant
15th Battalion K.O.Y.L.

Copies to :-
1 - C.O.
2 - Adjutant
3 - War Diary
4 - File
5 - A Coy
6 - B - "
7 - C - "
8 - D - "
9 - RSM.
10 - TO
11 - QM
12 - M.O.
13 - 120th Infy Bde.

War Diary

Appendix no 13

(4)

During the 25th August no active operations were undertaken but the day was devoted to consolidating the positions which had already been gained.

Appendix no 15

(8)

On the 26th August a Conference was held at rear Head-quarters at which orders were issued by the Brigadier-General Commanding for operations on the following day. On that day the intention was that the 119th Brigade should advance under barrage astride the BECKET CORNER - BISHOP'S CORNER Road, and having made their objective should mop up the area west of that road as far as own positions. Later this was extended so as to include BOWERY COTTAGES in the mopped up area. The duty of the 15th K.O.Y.L.I was to advance their right Company so as to meet the troops of the 119th Brigade advancing towards them, and the 164th Brigade on our right were also to attack.

It was decided to allot this task to "D" Company under CAPT. LINDEMERE, as this Company had not previously been engaged. As a consequence of this decision, "C" Company at CORNET PERDU was ordered to relieve "D" Company on the left out-post line. On relief "D" Company took the place of "B" Company on the right of the line, and "B" Company again fell back to CORNET PERDU.

Shortly before the attack took place orders were received to the effect that our front was extended by some 200 yards to the right as the 164th Brigade were unable to cover the area allotted to them. As a consequence of this it became necessary to allot a portio of our front to "C" Company, although this Company had been engaged shortly before. These adjustments were carried out on the night of the 26th/27th.

Appendix no 16 COPY No 3

15th Battalion King's Own
Yorkshire Light Infantry
Order No 10
by
Lieut Col T. W. T. ISAAC Commanding
26.8.1918

1. The enemy is holding the line of the LAUDICK from L 2 c. 1 1 through BOWERY COTTAGES to RUE MONTIGNY. It is proposed to turn this position from the North.

2. On a date and hour to be notified later the 119th Brigade will attack in a S.E. direction on both sides of the BECKET CORNER – BISHOPS CORNER Rd. The 61st Division will extend the objective through RUE PROVOST.

3. When the road has been made good as far south as BISHOPS CORNER 2 Companies of the 119th Brigade will turn westwards and mop up the area between the road and the LAUDICK including the BISHOPS CORNER – DENVER ROAD. In addition a special party will be told off to capture BOWER COTTAGES from the North. This attack will be carried out under a creeping barrage.

4. In addition to the creeping barrage there will be a standing barrage [illegible] with smoke on the LAUDICK from L 1 b 65 [illegible] to L 4 b 77. The barrage will remain on this line until [illegible] + [illegible] when it will stop. [illegible] will also be [illegible] on the road [illegible] through L 2 [illegible] the attack progresses.

5. At 3 am on 27th Aug. all troops east of the [illegible] Railway [illegible] will be withdrawn to the West of the Railway in order to avoid our barrage. These troops will move forward again after the barrage has lifted. The greatest care must be exercised by E & [illegible] Companies [illegible] where troops of the 119th Brigade are mopping up in front of [illegible] [illegible] of the [illegible] [illegible] [illegible] they must be [illegible] [illegible] the mopping up parties [illegible]

(2)

6. At Zero + 90 D Company of 1st ROYAL [illegible] will advance from the direction of DENVER with their left flank on the DENVER – BISHOPS CORNER Road and their right flank in touch with the 6th Division on the Southern boundary and will take over the line BOWERY COTTAGES – RUE PROVOST – BISHOPS CORNER making good any portion of this line that moppers up have been unable [illegible]. Lot [illegible] Section of the [illegible] Guns will be detailed to deal with isolated enemy posts in the houses along the [illegible].

7. The closest liaison must be kept between D Company and the 18th Brigade who will move forward on our right flank.

8. The method of advance will be by platoons in Artillery formation preceded by strong fighting patrols.

9. Water bottles will be filled and the unexpended portion of the days rations will carried on the man. The platoon of the Company in reserve will carry forward all available [illegible] and arrangements will be made for a further supply to be taken up.

10. O.C. C Company will hold himself in readiness to render any assistance to D Company that may be required.

11. The Signal that the various objectives have been taken will be three White Very Lights fired in quick succession.

12. Prisoners of War Post will be established at GRENADE FARM E 20 b 1.6. D Company will send prisoners to [illegible] Company who will provide escort.

13. If the objective is reached and the situation permits [illegible] Battalion will be withdrawn on 2/2-4-1 night.

14. R.A.P. will remain at [illegible]

15. ACKNOWLEDGE

(Sd) L. W. Sanderson
Major & a/Adjut
[illegible] Battalion

COPIES TO

1 – C.O.
2 – Adjutant
3 – War Diary
4 – File
5 – A Coy
6 – B
7 – C
8 – D
9 – R.S.M.
10 – T.O.
11 – Q.M.
12 – H.Q. [illegible] Bde
13 – [illegible] Bde
14 – [illegible] Bn & Brooks
15 – 10th R.S.B.
16 – [illegible] T.M.B.
17 – M.G.C.

War Diary

SECRET. Appendix no 17 Copy No. 4

15th Battalion King's Own Yorkshire Light Infantry

Amendments to Order No. 10.

26 - 8 - 18

1. Ref. Para. 6, the right boundary of "D" Company will be the light railway from L. 7. d. 95. 95 to L. 9. a. 3. 3, and the final front will be from BISHOP'S CORNER to L. 9. a. 3. 3.
   In consequence of this extension the right platoon of "C" Company will be responsible for taking the road from DENVER to L. 2. C. 8. 7, including 100 yards to the south of it. This platoon will remain under the orders of O.C. "C" Company.

2. A contact aeroplane will call for flares over the objective any time after Z + 2 hours. The contact plane will be marked by two black panels on the back edge of the lower plane.

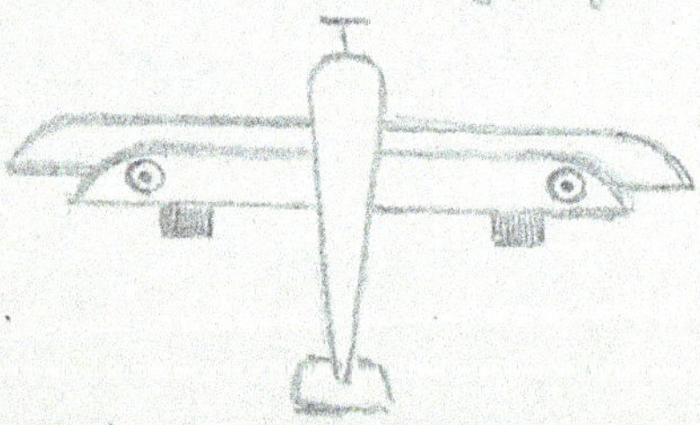

   Flares will be lit by the troops when the aeroplane calls for them with Klaxon Horn or light Signals.

3. Prisoners will be sent at once to SPEARMINT CORNER (not Grenade Farm as arranged) under escort, where they will be taken over by A.P.M. No documents will be taken off men. Officers' documents will be taken off them, but forwarded with the escort.

4. Care will be taken that troops do not expose themselves prior to zero hour.
   Zero hour will be 10 a.m. on 27th inst.

(Signed) L. M. Sanderson.
Major and A/Adjt.
15th Battalion, K.O.Y.L.I.

Copies to all recipients of Order No 10.

 Appendix no 18

At 10 a.m. on the 27th August, the 119th Brigade began their operations, and at 11-30 a.m., the hour fixed, "D" Company, 15th K.O.Y.L.I. began their advance, together with one platoon of "C" Company on their left. As the latter had no officer, CAPT. GARROD conducted its operations in person. Patrols from "D" Company succeeded in advancing a considerable distance, but as our troops on the right were again unable to make progress, and as "D" Company itself was met with heavy machine gun fire, they did not advance their main line. The platoon of "C" Company succeeded in advancing to L.2.c.5.8., the objective allotted to them, without meeting any troops of the 119th Brigade.

Information was subsequently received to the effect that the latter had only mopped up as far as L.2.d.9.9. CAPT. GARROD was therefore ordered to push on along the road until he effected a junction with them, supporting the platoon engaged with another platoon. This operation was successfully carried out, and a junction effected towards dusk.

On the evening of the 27th the line ran as follows:-
COCHIN CORNER - L.1.d.85.10, and thence along the road to L.2.d.9.9.

On the night of the 27th/28th "C" and "D" Companies, 11TH BATTALION CAMERON HIGHLANDERS, under Major Curtis and Capt. Lunn, were sent forward to relieve "C" and "D" Companies, 15TH BATTALION K.O.Y.L.I. On relief "C" Company fell back to a line about 200 yards west of the LAUDICK BROOK. "D" Company fell back to a line 200 yards west of the COCHIN CORNER - GENET CORNER Road.

SECRET. Appendix no 19 COPY No 7 28-8-18

1. By dawn 29th inst all troops of the 15th K.O.Y.L.I in the line will be relieved by the 11th Cameron Highlanders.

2. Relief for the forward Company of the K.O.Y.L.I. will not begin until after the attempt to gain the new objective tonight.

On completion of relief O.C 11th Bn. Cameron Highlanders will assume command of the sector & will hold the line with one Company from BISHOPS CORNER to L 2 C 8.6 — One Company just north of that line — One Company from the present junction with 184th Infantry Bde to L 2 C 8.6 — and One Company in support about K 12 b

A Company of the 15th K.O.Y.L.I, about L 1 will remain in its present position for the moment.

3. All arrangements will be made direct between C.Os. concerned.

4. Completion of relief will be wired to H.Qrs. by the word "SNOOKER"

5. In the event of the action tonight being successful the O.C 11th Cameron Hdrs. will take over the newly gained line & modify his dispositions accordingly.

6. ACKNOWLEDGE.

(Sgd) —
capt.
Brigade Major
120th Inf. Bde.

Issued through Signals at 6 pm.

Distribution:—

1 – G.O.C	9 – 120th T.M.B.
2 – Brigade Major	10 – 119th Bde
3 – Staff Capt.	11 – 184th "
4 – War Diary	12 – 40th Div. (G)
5 – File	13 – 165th Bde. R.F.A.
6 – 10th K.O.S.B.	14 – Bde Supply..
7 – 15th K.O.Y.L.I.	15 – " Signals
8 – 11th Camerons	

SECRET. *Appendix no 20* Copy No. 3.

15th Battalion King's Own Yorkshire L[ight] Infantry.

Order No. 11

by

Lt. Col. T.W.T. ISAAC, Commanding.

28 : 8 : 1918

1. The following Company Reliefs will be carried out on the night of 28th – 29th August, 1918:–

   "A" Co. Camerons will relieve "C" Co. K.O.Y.L.I.
   "B" Co. " " " "D" Co. "
   "D" Co. " " " "B" Co. "

   "C" Co. will not move until "A" Coy. Camerons have passed through them.
   "A" Co. K.O.Y.L.I. will remain in their present position.
   "B" Co. " " move to E. 27. c.
   "C" Co. " " " Reserve Line E. 25. d.
   "D" Co. " " " E. 25. a.

2. On being relieved "C" and "D" Companies will carry their own rations from ration dump, CORNET PERDU, to new position. "A" Co. will supply carrying party for "B" Co.

3. "C" Co. will provide 4 guides to be at Battalion H.Q. (Advanced) by 12 midnight, to guide "A" Co. Camerons to "C" Co. H.Q. (L.I.) "D" Co. guides will be at Advanced Battalion H.Q. at 11.30 p.m.

4. All maps will be handed over by platoon Commanders K.O.Y.L.I. to platoon Commanders 11th Camerons.

5. List of Trench Stores taken over will be [h]anded in to Battalion Orderly Room by 10 a.m. 29th inst.

6. Completion of relief will be reported to present Bn. H.Q. in the usual manner.

7. ACKNOWLEDGE.

N.B. Cos. to send 1 N.C.O. in advance to report to 2nd Lieut. JOLLEY at Rear H.Q.

Copies to:–

1. C.O.
2. Adjutant.
3. War Diary.
4. File.
5. "A" Co.
6. "B" Co.
7. "C" Co.
8. "D" Co.
9. R.S.M.
10. T.O.
11. Q.M.
12. M.O.
13. 120th Inf. Bde.

(Signed) L. M. Sanderson
Major and A/Adjt.
15th Battalion K.O.Y.L.I.

Ivan Deary

Appendix no 21

On the ~~29th~~ 28 August orders were received that two Companies of CAMERONS, and one Company K.O.Y.L.I. were to advance that evening and endeavour to gain the COCHIN CORNER - RUE PROVOST Road. Very little time was available for issuing orders, but a Conference was held at Company Headquarters at which it was decided that "C" and "D" Companies, CAMERONS, would move forward, and that "B" Company, K.O.Y.L.I., who had not suffered since the 15th August, should also attack on the right. Fighting patrols, followed by the Companies were to move out at 7 p.m., after heavy artillery had played on the likely points of resistance all day. About 7-30 p.m. reports were received from the two Companies of CAMERONS to the effect that they had been met by an enemy barrage, mixed with gas, and in consequence of this were unable to make any progress. In view of this CAPT. MORROW, who commanded "B" Company, decided not to advance his line, but sent out three strong patrols, who reported that the road as far as BOWERY COTTAGES, inclusive, was clear of the enemy, but that a machine gun post and snipers' post were active in the adjacent plantation. The line accordingly did not advance on that night.

About 2 a.m. on the ~~29th/30th~~ 28/29 August, the remaining Companies of the CAMERON HIGHLANDERS arrived, and the 15th K.O.Y.L.I. moved back to support.

During these operations a number of the enemy were killed and wounded, and 12 prisoners and 2 machine guns captured, one of the latter being left on the ground.

Appendix No 22

40th Division No. 901 (A).

H.Q., 31st Divnl. Artillery.
C.R.E., 40th Division.
O.C., 40th Divnl. Signal Coy.R.E.,
H.Q., 119th Infantry Brigade.
H.Q., 120th Infantry Brigade.
H.Q., 121st Infantry Brigade.
O.C., 104th Bn. Machine Gun Corps.
A.D.M.S., 40th Division.
D.A.P.M., 40th Division.
"G", 40th Division.

The following telegram has been received from the XV Corps Commander :-

"The Army Commander wishes me to convey to you his hearty congratulations on the success of your minor operation aaa Please also accept and convey to all concerned my own congratulations and appreciation of the good work performed."

The Divisional Commander wishes these congratulations, together with his own, conveyed to all who were concerned in the operations and compliments them on earning the approbation of the Army and Corps Commanders.

A. L. Bratton

Major,
D.A.A.G., 40th Division.

28/8/18.
(JM)

- 2 -

HEADQUARTERS, 120TH INFANTRY BRIGADE. No 120/474

120th Inf. Bde. No. 120/474.

10th Bn. K.O.S.B.
15th Bn. K.O.Y.L.I.
11th Bn. Cam. Highrs.
~~120th T.M. B.~~

In forwarding the above the Brigadier wishes to thank all those of this Brigade who were engaged in these operations for the excellent work they accomplished in this fighting.

Captain.
Staff Captain,
120th Infantry Brigade.

28-8-18.

SECRET. COPY NO..............

Appendix no. 23

15th Battalion KING,S OWN YORKSHIRE LIGHT INFANTRY.

ORDER NO 12.

by

MAJOR H. J. R. BOCK, COMMANDING

30th August 1918-

(1) The Battalion will move today to camp located at 27/U 24.c.2.4

(2) Companies will move off independently as follows:-

A. C. D. B. Headquarters.

Starting Point:- LA MOTTE CHURCH.

Time:, 2-15 p.m.

Dress:- Fighting Order. Steel Helmets will be worn, and S.B.Rs, carried at the "Alert".

200 yards interval will be maintained between platoons until west of the HAZEBROUCK - MORBECQUE ROAD, when Companies will close and march with five minutes interval between Companies.

(3) ROUTE TO BE FOLLOWED.

Road Junction D. 16.b.6.6. - Cross Roads D.3.c.8.4. (Sheet 36A)

Cross Roads V.26-d.6.4. - V. 25. Central. (Sheet 27)

(4) Company Field Kitchens and Lewis Gun Limbers will follow their Companies. Instructions regarding move of Transport Lines and Quartermaster's Stores have been issued to all concerned.

(5) The usual certificates regarding cleanliness and sanitation of present quarters will be rendered to Battalion Headquarters on arrival, together with Marching-in States.

(7) ACKNOWLEDGE.

(Signed) L. M. SANDISON.
Major & A/Adjutant,
15th Battalion, K.O.Y.L.I.

COPIES TO:-

1. C.O.
2. Adjutant.
3. War Diary.
4. File.
5. A. Company.
6. B. "
7. C. "
8. D. "
9. R.S.M.
10. T.O.
11. M.O.
12. Q.M.
13. 120th Infantry Brigade.

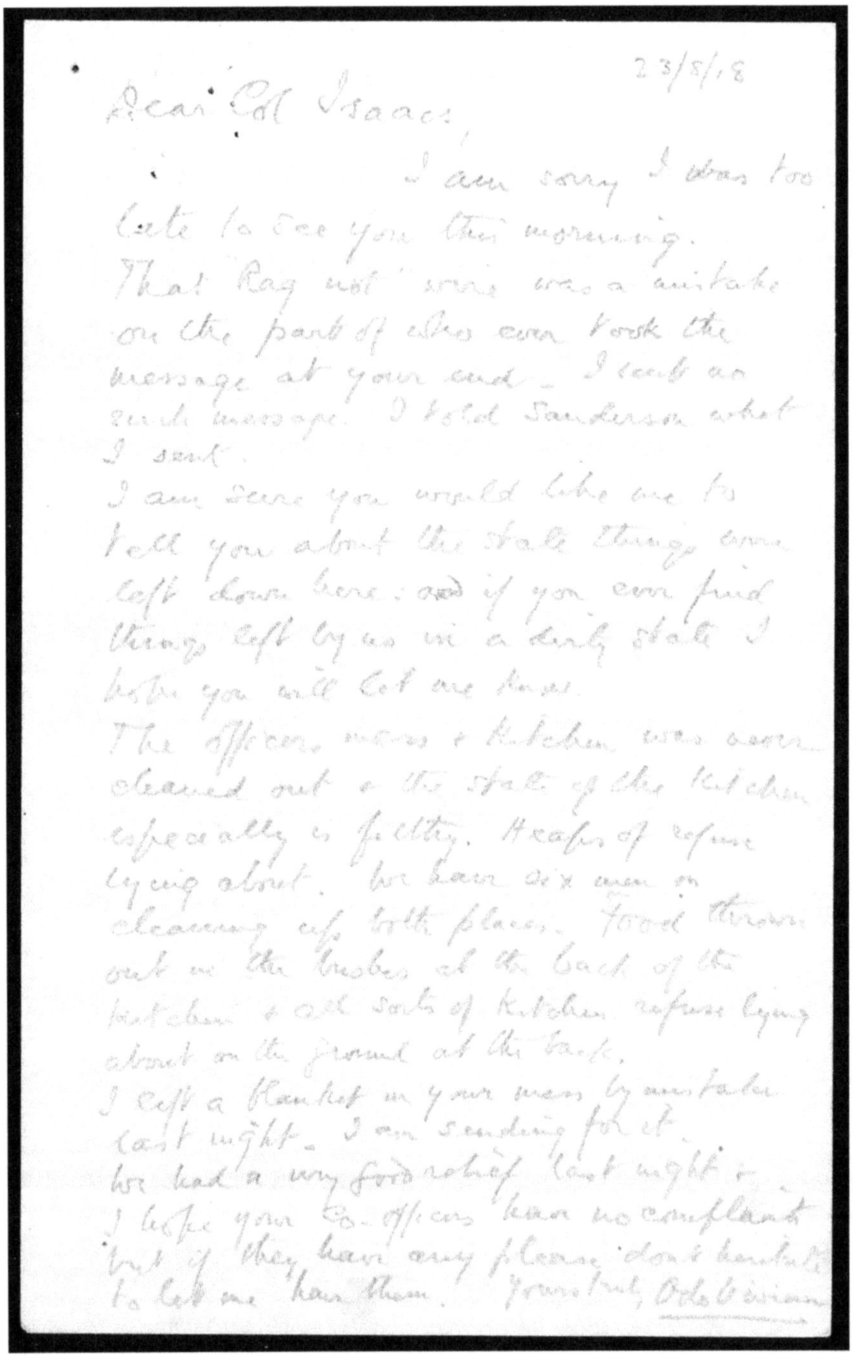
23/8/18

Dear Col Isaacs,

I am sorry I was too late to see you this morning.
That 'Rag not' wire was a mistake on the part of who ever took the message at your end. I sent no such message. I told Sanderson what I sent.
I am sure you would like me to tell you about the state things were left down here: and if you ever find things left by us in a dirty state I hope you will let me know.
The officers mess & kitchen was never cleaned out & the state of the kitchen especially is filthy. Heaps of refuse lying about. We have six men on cleaning up both places. Food thrown out in the bushes at the back of the kitchen & all sorts of kitchen refuse lying about on the ground at the back.
I left a blanket in your mess by mistake last night. I am sending for it.
We had a very good relief last night & I hope your Co. officers have no complaints but if they have any please don't hesitate to let me have them. Yours truly, Oda O'Brian

Appendix 24/8
No 24

Dear Colonel Vivian

Thank you for telling me about the state in which you found the River Camp. I much regret the matter & am very sorry you should have been so inconvenienced. We were moved into the Camp at very short notice, & were only there two nights. On the evening we left the G.O.C. held a Conference there which lasted till late & delayed our dinner. This may I hope be some excuse for the state of the kitchen. I had no time to inspect the camp myself tho' I personally saw my hut left clean. I enclose the marching out certificate which you may like to see. Evidently the kitchen was overlooked. Will you please return it. Truly Yours W.S. Dew

Copy Certificate

The HQ Lines of Lwa Camp were handed over in a clean and sanitary condition by FEPE

22.8.18

FEDE
Signed G Dakin Sgt.

Army Form C. 2121.
(In pads of 100.)

"A" Form.
MESSAGES AND SIGNALS.

No. of Message............

Prefix..........Code...........m.	Words. Charge.		Recd. at.........m.
Office of Origin and Service Instructions.	Sent	*This message is on a/c of:*	Date ....
	At ....m.	.... *Service.*	From ....
	To		
	By..............	(Signature of "Franking Officer.")	By ....

TO

Sender's Number.	Day of Month.	In reply to Number.	AAA
*			

From

Place

Time

The above may be forwarded as now corrected.	(Z)
Censor.	Signature of Addressor or person authorised to telegraph in his name.

* This line, except **AAA**, should be erased if not required.

Wt. W 3253/P511. 500,000 Pads. 1/18. B. & S. Ltd. **(E2389.)**

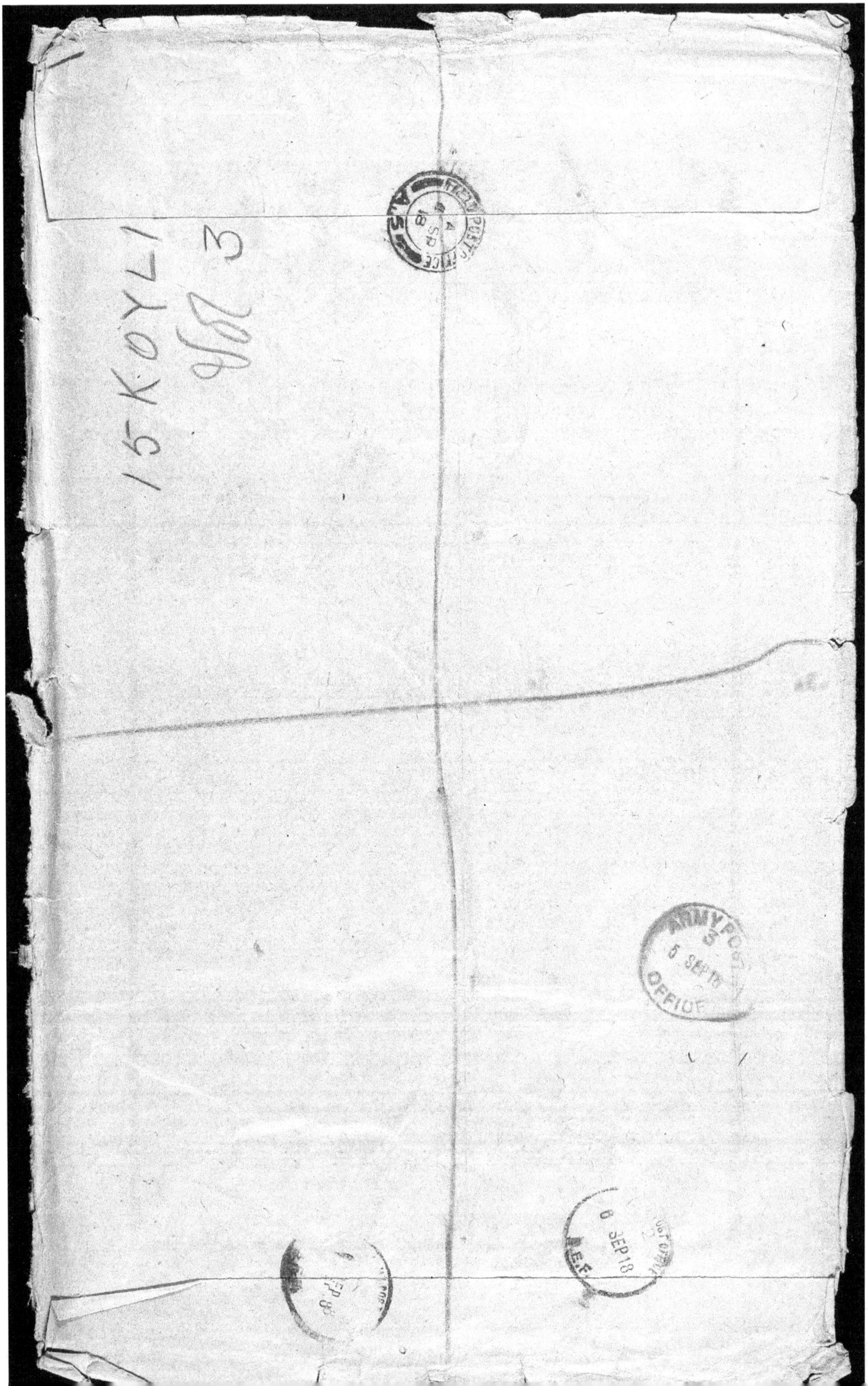
15 KOYLI
FIELD POST OFFICE
4 SEP 18
ARMY POST OFFICE
3
5 SEP 18
6 SEP 18
M.E.F.

4A

Vol 4

120/40

CONFIDENTIAL

WAR DIARY

OF

15th Battalion K.O.Y.L.I.

from 1st September 1918 to 30th September 1918

VOLUME (IV)

CONFIDENTIAL.

WAR DIARY

OF

15th BATTALION K·O·Y·L·I

FROM 1st SEPTEMBER 1918 TO 30th SEPTEMBER 1918

(VOLUME IV.)

[illegible] Major
for Lieut: Colonel
Commanding: 15th Battalion KOYLI

Volume No (iv) Sheet No 1. 15th Battalion K.O.Y.L.I. September 1918

Instructions regarding War Diaries and Intelligence Summaries are contained in F. S. Regs., Part II. and the Staff Manual respectively. Title pages will be prepared in manuscript.

WAR DIARY
or
INTELLIGENCE SUMMARY.
(Erase heading not required.)

Army Form C. 2118.

Place	Date	Hour	Summary of Events and Information	Remarks and references to Appendices
WALLON CAPPELL	1/9/18		Divine Service conducted by Chaplain Rev. E C Douglas. During the afternoon the Battn provided by Companies for baths	
"	2/9/18		Training under Company Commanders. Weather fine at intervals occasional showers.	
"	3/9/18		Battn Ceremonial Parade to prepare for following day	
"	4/9/18		Brigade Ceremonial Parade. Presentation of medals by MAJ GEN. PEYTON. Ptes WARD and CARTER (B Co) were presented with the Military medal for "Gallantry and devotion to duty displayed in action against the enemy on the 14/15 August 1918"	APPENDIX 1
"	5/9/18		Battn Field day carry out tactical scheme under MAJOR H. J. A. BOCK (C.O.)	
"	6/9/18		Brigade Field day. The Battn is in support during the whole of the operations.	
"	"	2pm	Battn Sports quite successful and enjoyed despite a very heavy thunderstorm during the afternoon	

A6945 Wt. W11422/M1160 350,000 12/16 D. D. & L. Forms/C./2118/14.

Volume (iv) Sheet No 2. 15th Battalion K.O.Y.L.I. September 1918

Army Form C. 2118.

Instructions regarding War Diaries and Intelligence Summaries are contained in F. S. Regs., Part II. and the Staff Manual respectively. Title pages will be prepared in manuscript.

WAR DIARY
or
INTELLIGENCE SUMMARY.
(Erase heading not required.)

Place	Date	Hour	Summary of Events and Information	Remarks and references to Appendices
WALLON CAPPEL	6/9/18	6pm	Lecture by BRIG GEN HOBKIRK on the mornings operation.	
"	7/9/18		Brigade Sports. The Battn spends the whole day at the Sports.	
"	8/9/18		Church Parade - Wet and dull weather.	
"	9/9/18		Training abandoned owing to wet weather - Conference with BRIG GEN HOBKIRK of Commanding Officers, Adjutants and Quartermasters. CAPT J.W.SWANSON returns from leave and takes over A/Adjutancy vice MAJOR L.M.SANDISON on course.	
"	10/9/18		Baths. Preparations for move tomorrow. MAJOR L M SANDISON away on course of instruction, CAPT. A. LINDEMERE assumes 2nd in command.	
"	11/9/18		Move by Motor lorries to Reserve Area. S.W. of STEENWERCK	APPENDIX 2
LUPIN FARM	12/9/18		Working parties provided	
"	13/9/18		The C.O., Adjutant & Company Commanders reconnoitered the Support line - (NIEPPE SWITCH) - At night move into this line and relieve 13th Inniskilling Fusiliers.	Appendix 3
POSTON FARM	14/9/18		Holding Support line - Wet weather - 3 Companies in the line and Bn at Battn HQ	
"	15/9/18		Holding line - during the afternoon & evening the Battn HQ	

A6945 Wt. W11422/M1160 350,000 12/16 D. D. & L. Forms/C./2118/14.

Volume (IV) Sheet No 3. 15th Battalion K.O.Y.L.I. September 1918

Army Form C. 2118.

WAR DIARY
or
INTELLIGENCE SUMMARY.
(*Erase heading not required.*)

Instructions regarding War Diaries and Intelligence Summaries are contained in F. S. Regs., Part II. and the Staff Manual respectively. Title pages will be prepared in manuscript.

Place	Date	Hour	Summary of Events and Information	Remarks and references to Appendices
POSTON FARM	15/9/18		are heavily shelled. At dusk move Battn HQ to HOLLEBEQUE	
			FARM. During the shelling our casualties were 1 O.R KILLED and	
			3 OR WOUNDED.	[initials]
HOLLEBEQUE FARM	16/9/18		At night take over Front line of Outposts from 10th K.O.S.B.	
			with all companies of the Battn in the Outpost line. EAST of	Appendix 4
TAFFY FARM			PONT-DE NIEPPE.	
	17/9/18		Holding Outpost line. Enemy Trench Mortar inflicts casualties	[initials]
			in C Co 1 OR Killed and 4 OR wounded.	[initials]
	18/9/18		During the day orders were received to reorganise the system	
			of Defence. A Conference of Company Commanders was held at	Appendix 5
			Battn HQ and at dusk A and D Co's took over the Outpost	
			line. B and C Co's taking up positions in the NIEPPE SYSTEM	
			Our casualties during the day were 1 OR Killed and 1 OR wounded.	
"	19/9/18		Holding Outpost line. casualties 1 O.R. Killed and 2 OR wounded	[initials]
			At night the Battn is relieved by the 11th Camerons and move	Appendix 6
			back to Reserve	[initials]

Volume (iv) Sheet No 4. 15th Battalion K.O.Y.L.I. September 1918

Army Form C. 2118.

WAR DIARY
or
INTELLIGENCE SUMMARY.
(*Erase heading not required.*)

Instructions regarding War Diaries and Intelligence Summaries are contained in F. S. Regs., Part II. and the Staff Manual respectively. Title pages will be prepared in manuscript.

Place	Date	Hour	Summary of Events and Information	Remarks and references to Appendices
LETT FARM	20/9/18		In Reserve. Weather now greatly improved. 1 O.R. wounded	[illegible]
"	21/9/18		Capt T.L. Webb takes over command of the Battn by order of the Brigadier. MAJOR H.J.R. BOCK relinquishes command.	[illegible]
"	22/9/18		A and D Companies shelled out of their quarters during the early morning. D Company having one casualty (wounded). At 9pm the Battn was relieved by 23rd LANCASHIRE FUSILIERS	[illegible] Appendix
LE VERRIER	23/9/18		Capt. A. LINDEMERE takes over command of the Battn	[illegible]
"	24/9/18		Training under Company arrangements.	
"	25/9/18		Training. MAJOR L.M. SANDISON returns from Paris and takes over command of Battn. CAPT T.L. WEBB acting Second in Command.	[illegible]
"	26/9/18		Training under good weather conditions.	
	27/9/18		MAJOR H.J.R. BOCK leaves the Battn. At noon strike camp and move into Brigade Reserve NORTH of STEENWERCK.	[illegible] Appendix 8
			Before moving C.O. inspects Companies (B & C)	[illegible]

A6945 Wt. W11422/M1160 350,000 12/16 D. D. & L. Forms/C./2118/14.

Volume (iv) Sheet-No 5.

15th Battalion K.O.Y.L.I.

September 1918.

Army Form C. 2118.

WAR DIARY
or
INTELLIGENCE SUMMARY.
(Erase heading not required.)

Instructions regarding War Diaries and Intelligence Summaries are contained in F. S. Regs., Part II. and the Staff Manual respectively. Title pages will be prepared in manuscript.

Place	Date	Hour	Summary of Events and Information	Remarks and references to Appendices
PADDY FARM	28/9/18		Weather bad rain & cold, very little training possible. CAPT E.J. GROVES M.C. of 1st CHESHIRE REGT arrives to take over Second in Command	
	29/9/18		A&D Companies inspected by C.O. Church parade.	
	30/9/18		Baths by Companies. Boxing and Football matches arranged for afternoon but postponed owing to bad weather.	

A6945 Wt. W11422/M1160 350,000 12/16 D. D. & L. Forms/C./2118/14.

Appendix I

BATTALION ORDERS No.[illegible]
by
MAJOR H.J.H.BACK
COMMANDING 15th BATTALION KING'S OWN YORKSHIRE LIGHT INFANTRY.

[illegible] ON CAMP [illegible] 3-9-1918

=-=

DETAIL.

Orderly Officer to-morrow,	2/Lieut. Sir [illegible] (Bart)
Next for duty,	2/Lieut. [illegible]
Company on duty to-morrow,	"A" Company
Next for duty,	"B" Company

[illegible]. ROUTINE.

Reveille will be at 6 a.m.
Breakfast " " " 6-30 a.m.

[illegible]. INSPECTION.

The Brigade will be inspected by the Divisional Commander in field at [illegible] to-morrow, when medal ribbons will be presented to the undermentioned:-

No. [illegible] Pte. [illegible] "[illegible]" Coy.
No. [illegible] Pte. [illegible] "[illegible]" Coy.

The Battalion will parade as strong as possible in camp at 7-15 a.m. under R.S.M. for equalising Companies.

Officers will join their Companies at 7-30 a.m. inspect and size their Companies, and tell them off into three platoons.

Dress:- Drill Order - S.A.A. will not be carried.

Right markers will report to R.S.M. at 7-40 a.m.

One left marker per Company, and one right marker from "A" Company will report to R.S.M. at Orderly Room at [illegible] a.m.

[illegible]. LECTURE.

All Officers and N.C.Os. of the rank of Sergeant and over will attend a lecture by Major [illegible] in the Theatre at [illegible] p.m. to-morrow.

[illegible]. DRESS.

Belts and S.D.Rs. will be worn by all ranks leaving camp.

(Signed) [illegible],
2/Lieut. & A/Adjt.
15th Battalion K.O.Y.L.I.

[illegible].

The Battalion Sports will be held on Friday and not Thursday as stated in Battalion Orders Sept. 1st.

The Divisional Concert Party will give a performance in this camp on Thursday at [illegible] p.m.

Appendix II

[illegible] 111

[illegible] Battalion [illegible] Light Infantry.

[illegible] No. 33.

by

Major [illegible] Commanding. [illegible]

Reference (1) The Battalion will move [illegible] Battalion [illegible] present occupation at A.21.[illegible] [illegible] Cross Roads at [illegible] Cross Roads at A.[illegible] [illegible] near the [illegible] the following order [illegible] Headquarters, "A", "B", [illegible] Companies. Companies will [illegible] strength return to [illegible]

(2) [illegible] [illegible] in addition to [illegible]

(3) [illegible] The following advance party will [illegible] [illegible] at [illegible] Battalion Headquarters [illegible] to be detailed by [illegible] and Transport [illegible] [illegible] men and [illegible] to be [illegible] advance party [illegible]

(4) [illegible]

(5) [illegible] Transport will [illegible]

(6) [illegible] to be at [illegible]

(7) [illegible]

(8) [illegible]

(9) [illegible] Headquarters [illegible] A. [illegible] Brigade [illegible]

(10) [illegible]

[illegible]

Copies to:-

1. [illegible]
2. A.[illegible]
3. Plts.
4. M.O.
5. Q.M.
6. T.O.
7. R.S.M
8.–11. O.C. A–D Coy
12. 120th Bde
13. H.Q. Mess
14. War Diary

Van Dainy

Appendix III

SECRET.

COPY No. 12

15th Battalion King's Own Yorkshire Light Infantry

OPERATION ORDER No. 15

by

Major H. J. R. BOCK. Commanding.

LUPIN FARM 13.9.18.

Ref. Maps 1/40000 36 N.W.

(1) The 15th Battalion K.O.Y.L.I. will relieve the 13th Inniskilling Fusiliers in the support area to-day.

"A" Company will relieve "E" Company Inniskillings
"B" " " " "G" " "
"C" " " " "F" " "
"D" " " " "H" " "

"B" Company will be in reserve at Bn. H.Qrs.

Companies will march off independently in the following order.

H.Qrs. "D" "C" "A" "B" Companies.

H.Qrs. marching off at 6-30 p.m. with 5 minutes interval between Companies. 3 minutes interval between Platoons after passing through STEENWERCQUE

DRESS:- Steel Helmets & S.B.R's at the "Alert". Great-coats to be carried on the back.
Water-bottles to be filled before marching off.

ROUTE:- A.22.a.4.8 – STEENWERCQUE ROAD – A.17.d.4.4 – A.18.c.3.3 – A.18.d.1.3 – B.19.a.2.1.
1 Officer and 1 guide per platoon will be in waiting at Cross Roads at B.19.a.2.1 at 7.45 p.m.

(2) All maps, photographs, defence schemes, etc. will be taken over and receipts forwarded to Battalion H.Qrs. as soon as possible after relief.

Companies will forward to Battalion H.Qrs. by 12-noon on the 15th a sketch map showing dispositions by platoons.

(3) Completion of relief to be reported to Battalion H.Qrs. as already arranged.

(4) LEWIS GUNS

20 Lewis Guns will be taken into the line as detailed by the Lewis Gun Officer. The remainder will be dumped at present Battalion H.Qrs. Lewis Gun limbers will follow Companies.

(5) The following will be dumped at Battalion H.Qrs. by 4 p.m. to-day, for transport to Q.M. Stores:-

Packs, Officers' valises; Company mess boxes; Blankets in bundles of 10, and all surplus Company Stores.

(6) COOKING. -

Cookers will proceed to new Transport lines after tea today.

The 4 cooker dixies per Company will be taken forward to the trenches with rations.

(7) RATIONS.

Rations will be delivered at the following points tonight at 12-30 a.m.:-

"A" Company	-	ORVILLE JUNCTION
"C" "		THUNDER COPPS
"D" "		TAFFY FARM.
"B" "		BATTALION H.Qrs.

Water-carts will call during the afternoon.

(8) LOCATIONS.

Battalion H.Qrs.	POSTOON FARM - B.30.b.4.0.
Transport lines.	SCANLON CROSS. A.22.d.5.9
Quartermaster's Stores	
Brigade H.Qrs.	LOWER FARM. A.24.c.6.8. (10 a.m. 14th)
Regimental Aid Post	→ near Battalion H.Qrs.
Advanced Dressing Station.	A24.d.2.1
Cemetery,	PONT D'ACHELES.

(9) ACKNOWLEDGE

(Signed) T. W. SWANSON
Capt & A/Adjutant,
15th Battalion, K.O.Y.L.I.

COPIES TO:-

1. - C.O.	8. - Q.M.
2. - Adjutant.	9. - T.O.
3. - File	10. - M.O.
4. - "A" Company	11. - R.S.M.
5. - "B" "	12. - 120th Bde
6. - "C" "	13. - 13th Inniskillings
7. - "D" "	

O C Inniskilling

ANNEXURE IV

To be rendered to Officers i/c Records for transmission to the War Office. Army Form B. 158.

CAVALRY, ARTILLERY and INFANTRY only.

SECRET. Copy No. ....

Regiment, etc., or Depot 15th Battalion King's Own Yorkshire Light Infantry

Station

Date

OPERATION ORDER – No. 16.

by

Major H. J. R. BOCK, Commanding.

LIST OF OFFICERS.

16-9-18.

Reference map. 1/20,000. 36 N.W.

(1) The Battalion will be relieved in the support area by the 11th Camerons tonight.

"D" Company Camerons will relieve "A" Co. KOYLI

"B" " " " "C" " "

"A" " " " "B" " "

"C" " " " "D" " "

One officer per Company & one guide per platoon will be at Cross Roads near Owl FARM at [illegible] to guide up the Camerons.

(2) On relief the 15th K.O.Y.L.I. will relieve 10th K.O.S.B. in the front line under arrangements to be made between O.C. Companies concerned.

"A" Company KOYLI will relieve "F" Co. K.O.S.B.

"C" " " " "E" " "

"D" " " " "G" " "

"B" " " " "E" " "

(3) Completion of relief will be reported to Bn. H. Qrs. as arranged.

All photographs etc. will be taken over, & list of Trench Stores forwarded to Bn. H. Qrs. as soon as possible after the relief.

Sketch maps showing dispositions down to platoons must reach H.Qrs. by 4 p.m. on 17th.

(4) **RATIONS**. The arrangements for delivery of rations tonight have been communicated to all concerned.

(5) **COMMUNICATION**. The Corps Commander directs that in front of Bn. H. Qrs.:–

(a) The telephone will only be used for the transmission of messages in cases of emergency & by no one under the rank of officer.

(b) Only messages of an urgent nature will be sent by Buzzer, & these must invariably be coded.

(6) **LOCATIONS**:–

Battalion H. Qrs.	TAFFY FARM
Transport Lines. Q.M. Stores	SCANLON CROSS
Brigade H.Qrs.	LOWER FARM.
Refill. Pt. (?)	B.21.a.6.2
Cemetery	PONT D'ACHELLES.

(7) ACKNOWLEDGE

Copies To:–

1 – C.O.		9 – T.O.	
2 – Adjt.		10 – M.O.	
3 – [illegible]		11 – R.S.M.	
4-7 – "A" – "D" Cos.		12 – O.C. Bn. H.Q.C.	
8 – Q.M.		13 – 120th Bde.	
		14 – [illegible]	
		15 – 10th K.O.S.B.	

[illegible signature]
Capt. & Adjt.
15th Bn. K.O.Y.L.I.

Printed form headings on the page (largely overwritten): Married or Single; Officers on duty with the Unit; Date of ...; Station if on detachment; Lieut.-Colonel—; Majors—; Captains—; Lieutenants—; 2nd Lieutenants—; Adjutant—; Quartermaster—; Riding Master—; WARRANT OFFICERS.; Master Gunner; Serjeant-Major; Bandmaster; OFFICERS ATTACHED (Including Reserve and Territorial Force Officers.); Authority ...; Rank | Name | Corps | Authority | Date of joining

* The letter "M" or "S" is to be placed before the names of Officers.
† For Units of Royal Artillery, Depots of all Arms and Special Reserve Units.
NOTE 1.—The word "Sick" to be inserted against the names of all Officers who are on the Sick List, and the words "Assistant Adjutant," "Instructor of Gunnery," &c., against the name of an Officer holding such an appointment.
NOTE 2.—This Return should be rendered in Duplicate by units of New Armies only.

[1601] W2864/P419 300m 12/17ss 145 G & S 57 Forms B. 158 / 9

To be rendered to Officers i/c Records for transmission to the War Office. Army Form B. 158.

SECRET Copy No. ----

CAVALRY, ARTILLERY and INFANTRY only.

1st Battalion, King's Own Yorkshire Light Infantry

Regiment, etc., or Depot **DEFENCE INSTRUCTION No. 1.**

Station by

Major H. J. R. Bock, Commanding.

Date 18.9.18.

LIST OF OFFICERS.

Married or Single	Officers doing duty with the Unit NAME	Date of joining the Unit	Stations (if on detachment)

Ref. map 36 N.W. 1/20,000.

(1) The defensive arrangements of the Brigade front (STEENWERCK sector) will be organised as follows:-

Lieut.-Colonel—

(2) **SCHEME.**

Majors—

(a) The outpost line will be held by one Battalion with two Companies in the outpost line, and two Companies in the NIEPPE system.

Captains—

(b) One Battalion will be in support with two Companies in the ESTAIRES-LYS line, and 2 Companies in Shelter & trenches.

(c) One Battalion in Reserve about the road through B.19.c. and B.25.a.

Lieutenants—

(3) **ACTION IN CASE OF HOSTILE ATTACK.**

(a) In the event of hostile attack the main Line of Resistance will be the ESTAIRES-LYS line as far north as B.28.b.9.5. thence to the NIEPPE SYSTEM, to the Brigade Northern ~~Sector~~ boundary.

(b) The outpost troops will fight as long as possible on the outpost line but will not be reinforced.

(c) The main Line of Resistance will be maintained at all costs.

2nd Lieutenants—

(d) The Line of Resistance will be continued to the South along old British trenches in C.13.d. & C.13.b.

All Officers will make themselves thoroughly acquainted with the defences of the main Line of Resistance, the approaches to this line, & the best lines for counter attack. All Officers must know action to be taken in the event of attack.

Adjutant—

Quartermaster—

(4) **DISPOSITIONS.**

Riding Master—

The new dispositions will come into force tonight 18/19th.

WARRANT OFFICERS.

The Battalion sector will be as follows:-

Master Gunner—

OUTPOST LINE. From B.29.a.1.9. To B.17.c.8.7.

Serjeant-Major—

SUPPORT LINE. " B.28.b.9.5 " B.16.b.9.2.

Bandmaster—

OFFICERS ATTACHED.

(5) The outpost line will be occupied by "A" and "D" Companies as follows:-

(Including Special Reserve and Territorial Force Officers.)

Authority—

"A" Company. From B.29.a.1.9. To B.23.d.8.7 (exclusive)

"A" Co. Hd. Qrs. at B.23.a.9.3.

"D" Company. From B.23.d.8.7 (inclusive) with post at present occupied by "C" Co. To B.17.c.9.7.

"D" Co. H. Qrs. at B.23.b.2.3.

Rank	Name	Corps	Date of joining

* The letter "M" or "S" is to be placed before the names of Officers.
† For Units of Royal Artillery, Depots of all Arms and Special Reserve Units.
NOTE 1.—The word "Sick" to be inserted against the names of all Officers who are on the Sick List, and the words "Assistant Adjutant," "Instructor of Gunnery," &c., against the name of an Officer holding such an appointment.
NOTE 2.—This Return should be rendered in Duplicate by units of New Armies only.

[1601] W2864/P419 300m 12/17 145 G & S 57 Forms B. 158 / 9

To be rendered to Officers i/c Records for transmission to the War Office. Army Form B. 158.

(2)

CAVALRY, ARTILLERY and INFANTRY only.

NIEPPE SYSTEM. will be occupied as follows:—

Regiment, etc., and Depot "C" Company. From B.28.b.9.5 To B.22.b.5.6 (inclusive)
"C" Co. Hd. Qrs. at B.28.b.3.8.

Station "B" Company From B.22.b.5.6 (exclusive)
To – B.16.d.9.2 (inclusive)

Date

LIST OF OFFICERS.

"B" Co. Hd. Qrs. at B.16.d.6.0.

(6) Companies will move to their new dispositions at 9.30 pm.

* Married or Single	Officers doing duty with the Unit NAME	Date of being taken on the strength of the Unit†	Stations (if on detachment)

(7) Companies will wire to Battalion Hd. Qrs. as soon as new dispositions have been adopted, using the code word "WHISKY."

Lieut.-Colonel—

List of Trench Stores taken over will be forwarded to Battalion H.Qrs. as soon as possible & a sketch map of new dispositions down to platoons will be forwarded to Battalion Hd. Qrs. not later than 10 am. tomorrow.

Majors—

Captains—

(8) SANITATION.

Latrine buckets are being sent to Companies tonight. Companies will ensure that they are made fly proof locally.

Lieutenants—

(9) S.A.A. Indents for S.A.A. required to be rendered to Battalion Hd. Qrs. as soon as possible.

(10) LOCATIONS.

Battalion Hd. Qrs.
Transport Lines.
Q.M. Stores
Aid Post
} As at present.

2nd Lieutenants—

Cemetery – – – – LE GRAND BEAUMARD.

(11) ACKNOWLEDGE.

(Signed) J. W. Swanson
Capt. & A/Adjt.
15th Bn. K.O.Y.L.I.

COPIES TO:–

Adjutant— 1 – Co.
Quartermaster— 2 – File
Riding Master— 3–6 – "A"–"D" Coys.

WARRANT OFFICERS.

7 – M.O.
Master Gunner— 8 – Q.M.
Serjeant-Major— 9 – T.O.
Bandmaster— 10 – Intell. Officer & L.G.O.

OFFICERS ATTACHED.

11 – R.E.
12 – 120th Bde.
13 – 11th Camerons.

(Including Special Reserve and Territorial Force Officers. Authority to be quoted.)

Rank	Name	Corps	Authority	Date of joining

* The letter "M" or "S" is to be placed before the names of Officers.
† For Units of Royal Artillery, Depots of all Arms and Special Reserve Units.
NOTE 1.—The word "Sick" to be inserted against the names of all Officers who are on the Sick List, and the words "Assistant Adjutant," "Instructor of Gunnery," &c., against the name of an Officer holding such an appointment.
NOTE 2.—This Return should be rendered in Duplicate by units of New Armies only.

[1601] W2864/P419 300m 12/17 ss 145 G & S 57 Forms B. 158 / 9

Officers absent on duty.

(Exclusive of seconded Officers, but including Officers posted and not joined.)

Married	Rank and Name	On what duty, at what station, from what time

Officers and Warrant Officers absent with Leave.

	Rank and Name	By whose authority and date of order			Since what time

Officers and Warrant Officers who have *joined* during the preceding month, showing whether from leave of absence, on appointment, &c.

	Rank and Name	Date and cause

Officers and Warrant Officers who have *quitted* during the preceding month, showing whether on leave of absence, removal, death, &c.

	Rank and Name	Date and cause

Officers absent without leave.

Rank and Name	Since what time

____________________ Commanding.

Appendix VI

To be rendered to Officers i/c Records for transmission to the War Office. Army Form B. 158.

CAVALRY, ARTILLERY and INFANTRY only.

Regiment, etc., or Depot

Station SECRET. COPY No. . . .

15th Battalion, King's Own Yorkshire Light Infantry.

Date

LIST OF OFFICERS.

OPERATION ORDER No. 17.

by Major H. G. R. Brook, Commanding.

19. 9. 18

Ref. Map. 36 NW. 1/20,000.

(1) The Battalion will be relieved in the front line by the 11th Camerons tonight under arrangements to be made between the Company Commanders concerned.

"A" Company Camerons will relieve "B" Company, K.O.Y.L.I.
"B" " " " " "C" " "
"C" " " " " "D" " "
"D" " " " " "A" " "

(2) ROUTE—

(b) Soup Kitchen – OWL FARM, across country to Cross Roads at B.19.a.3.1 where Company Q.M. Sergts. will await to guide Companies in.

(a) On relief the K.O.Y.L.I. will take over the billets in the Reserve Area at present occupied by the 10th K.O.S.B., under arrangements to be made by the Q.M.

(3) Completion of Reliefs to be reported to Bn. Hd. Qrs.

All photographs, etc., will be handed over. List of Trench Stores handed over to be sent to Battalion Hd. Qrs. by 12 noon on the 20th.

(4) SOUP.

Men may obtain soup from Soup Kitchen in their canteens as Companies pass.

(5) LEWIS GUN LIMBERS – will be at last night's ration points at midnight. Companies will leave a Lewis Gunner N.C.O. in charge of Company Lewis Guns if relieved before arrival of Lewis Gun Limbers.

(6) OFFICERS' CHARGERS.

Company Commanders' horses will be at OWL FARM at 11 p.m. If not required wire Bn. Hd. Qrs.

(7) FOOD. Water-carts & cookers will be at new camp & a hot meal will be served to Companies on arrival. Officers' valises will be brought up.

(8) LOCATIONS.

Battalion H. Qrs.	LETT FARM.
Transport Lines } Q.M. Stores }	SCANLON CROSS.
Bde Hd. Qrs.	LOWER FARM
Cemetery	LE GRAND BEAUMART.

(9) ACKNOWLEDGE.

(Sgd) J. W. SWANSON.
Capt & A/Adjt.
15th Bn, K.O.Y.L.I.

Copies to:-
1 – C.O.
2 – Adjt.
3 – File
4–7 – "A" – "D" Coys.
8 – Q.M.
9 – T.O.
10 – M.O.
11 – R.S.M.
12 – 120th Bde.
13 – 11th Camerons
14 – 10th K.O.S.B.

* The letter "M" or "S" is to be placed before the names of Officers.
† For Units of Royal Artillery, Depots of all ... and Special Reserve Units.
NOTE 1.—The word "Sick" to be inserted against the names of all Officers who are on the Sick List, and the words "Assistant Adjutant," "Instructor of Gunnery," &c. against the name of an Officer holding such appointment.
NOTE 2.—This Return should be rendered in duplicate by units of New Armies only.

[1601] W2864/P419 300m 12/14 ... 145 H & S ... Forms B. 158 / 9

Officers absent on duty.

(Exclusive of seconded Officers, but including Officers posted and not joined.)

Married or Single	Rank and Name	On what duty, at what station, from what time

Officers and Warrant Officers absent with Leave.

Rank and Name	By whose permission, and date of order	On what account	From what time	To what time

Officers and Warrant Officers who have *joined* during the preceding month, showing whether from leave of absence, on appointment, &c.

Rank and Name	Date and cause

Officers and Warrant Officers who have *quitted* during the preceding month, showing whether on leave of absence, removal, death, &c.

Rank and Name	Date and cause

Officers absent without leave.

Rank and Name	Since what time

_______________ Commanding.

SECRET.......... Appendix VII COPY NO. 8....

15th BATTALION, KING'S OWN YORKSHIRE LIGHT INFANTRY.

OPERATION ORDER NO. 18.
by
CAPTAIN T. L. WEBB, Commanding.

21-9-18.

Reference Map 1/20,000 MERRIS (combined)

(1) The Battalion will be relieved in the Reserve Area by the 23rd LANCASHIRE FUSILIERS to-morrow night, 22nd/23rd, and will proceed after relief to the Reserve Area at PONT WEMEAU.
Relief will take place between 9 and 12 p.m., and Co. Commanders will report relief complete before marching off.

(2) ORDER OF MARCH.
"C" Company: "D" Company: "A" Company: "B" Company: Battalion Headquarters.
Five minutes interval between Companies, and three minutes interval between platoons until the Battalion has passed LE GRAND BEAUMART.
DRESS:- Steel Helmets; S.B.Rs. at "Alert" position.
ROUTE:- B.18.a.3.1: A.18.d.1.3: STEENWERCK.
A.22.a.3.7: A.20.b.2.4:
F.24.d.7.1: F.24.c.3.0, where one guide per Company, under CAPT. MORROW, will be in waiting to guide the Battalion in.

(3) LEWIS GUN LIMBERS - will follow Companies.

(4) ARRIVAL. On arrival in new Camp Co. Commanders will report to C.O. at Battalion Headquarters (F.23.d.9.3.) that their Companies have arrived in billets.

(5) FOOD. Tea will be served to Companies on arrival.

(6) COMPANY COMMANDERS' HORSES - will be at A.18.d.1.3. at 9-30 p.m.

(7) OFFICERS' VALISES. O.C. "B" and "D" Companies will arrange for Officers' valises of these Companies to be conveyed on "B" or "D" Companies' Lewis Gun Limbers.
O.C. "A" and "C" Companies will make similar arrangements.
Lewis Gun Limbers will arrive at Company H.Q. at 8 p.m..

(8) ADVANCE PARTY. This has been detailed separately.

(9) TRENCH STORES,ETC. Defence Instructions and aeroplane photographs will be handed over on relief. List of Trench Stores handed over will be forwarded to Battalion Headquarters by 12 noon on the 23rd inst..
Receipts for Defence Instructions and aeroplane photographs will be forwarded to Battalion Headquarters at the same time.

(10) LOCATIONS.

Battalion Headquarters.......	F.23.d.9.3. 7 29 a 40 98
Q.M. Stores..................	F.23.d.1.2.
Transport Lines..............	-ditto-
Brigade Headquarters.........	WINK COTTAGE, (after 10 a.m. on the 23rd inst)

(11) ACKNOWLEDGE.

(Signed) J.W.SWANSON,
Capt. & A/Adjutant.
15th Battalion, K.O.Y.L.I.

COPIES TO:-
1. C.O.
2. Adjt.
3. File.
4 - 7 "A" - "D" Cos.
8 Q.M.
9. T.O.
10. M.O.
11. R.S.M.
12. I.O. & O.C. Bn. H.Q. Co.
13. 120th Bde.

File

BATTALION ORDERS No.76. Appendix VIII

by

MAJOR L. M. SANDISON,

Commanding, 15th Battalion, King's Own Yorkshire Light Infantry.

In the Field. 27-9-18.

DETAIL.

Orderly Officer to-morrow.......... 2/Lieut. S.SCARR, M.C.
Next for duty...................... " S.DAWSON.
Company on duty to-morrow.......... "A" Company.
Next for duty...................... "B" "

339. ROUTINE.

Routine will be the same as for to-day.

340. C.O's INSPECTION.

The C.O. will inspect Companies as follows:-

"D" Company........ 9-0 a.m.
"A" " .... 9-45 "

Companies will parade as strong as possible, and will be formed up on Company Parade Grounds in close column of platoons, two paces interval between sections.

DRESS:- Fighting order.

Lewis Gunners will parade with Companies.

341. DISCIPLINE.

The Battalion is now in the Gas "Alert" Zone. All ranks will wear Steel Helmets in present location.

342. TRAINING.

(A) Lewis Gunners. Except during C.O's Inspection and S.B.R. Inspection Lewis Gunners will carry on training to-morrow as usual from 9-0 a.m. to 12-0 noon under Sergt. P. PEARSON.

(B) Inspection. The Brigade Gas N.C.O. will inspect the Small Box Respirators of the Battalion to-morrow as follows:-

"A" Company........ 9-0 a.m.
"B" " .... 9-30 "
"C" " .... 9-50 "
"D" " .... 10-30 "
Battalion H.Q... 10-45 "

Companies will parade as strong as possible on Company Parade Grounds at these times.

Lewis Gunners will attend these parades.

(C) After the C.O's Inspection and S.B.R. Inspection to-morrow, Companies will be at the disposal of Company Commanders.

343. RETURN.

O.C. Companies will render to Orderly Room by 9-0 a.m. on the 29th September a Nominal Roll of all men serving under their command who are experienced farm labourers.

344. FOOD POISONING.

A.R.O. 2257 d/24-9-18 is republished for information:-

"A.R.O 2197 is cancelled and the following substituted:-

In order to minimize the risk of outbreaks of food poisoning, meat-pies, rissoles and sausages, hashes,etc., made from previously cooked food, should be consumed immediately after being re-cooked. These dishes may be prepared overnight, but must under no circumstances be cooked until the following day. Tinned food should be consumed immediately after being opened.

Food should be carefully protected against flies, and on no account be stored in dining-halls.

Scrupulous cleanliness must be observed in cook-houses, both as regards cooking utensils and personnel: the importance of washing their hands after visiting the latrines, and before handling food, should be impressed on cooks. No man who has suffered from interic fever, dysentery, or any other gastro-intestinal trouble, should be employed in a cook-house, and men who are thus employed should be instructed to report sick at once if suffering from diarrhoea, no matter how slight the attack may be".

(Signed) J.W.SWANSON,
Captain & A/Adjutant.
15th Battalion, K.O.Y.L.I.

Adjt

5A

Vol 5

(Secret)

War Diary

of

15th Bn. King's Own Yorkshire Light Infantry

From 1st October 1918 To 31st October 1918

Volume No. 5

SECRET.

15 Battn
K.O.Y.L.I.

October 1918

Volume No 5

Instructions regarding War Diaries and Intelligence Summaries are contained in F. S. Regs., Par. II. and the Staff Manual respectively. Title pages will be prepared in manuscript.

WAR DIARY
or
INTELLIGENCE SUMMARY.
(Erase heading not required.)

Army Form C. 2118.

1

Place	Date	Hour	Summary of Events and Information	Remarks and references to Appendices
NIEPPE	1/10/18		Preparations for the line. at 7 pm. march off and relieve 23rd CHESHIRE REGT in the front line	APPENDIX 1
"	2/10/18		LT COL. T.W.T. ISAACS rejoined from leave to U.K. Owing to the enemy retiring and the other Battalions of the Brigade pushing forward, the Battn is now in support.	
"	3/10/18		MAJOR L.M. SANDISON left Battn to attend Senior Officers Course at Aldershot England	
"	4/10/18		The Battn provided 200 men for working parties to fill up large craters at ERQUINGHEM.	
ARMENTIERES	5/10/18		Relieved the 13th E. LANCS in another Support area. Winter time came into force at midnight 5th-6th and clocks were put back one hour at 1 am 6th	APPENDIX 2
"	6/10/18		Front line is withdrawn & present Support line held by the Battn becomes the front line. Enemy shelled our line and H.Qrs heavily for 1 hour at dawn.	

A6945 Wt. W11422/M1160 350,000 12/16 D. D. & L. Forms/C./2118/14.

Six Officers join the Battn from England; 2nd Lieuts. Fox, Pugh, Siddle, Battersby, Yorkstone, Moore.

15th Bn. R.O.Y.L.I. October 1918

Volume No 5

Instructions regarding War Diaries and Intelligence Summaries are contained in F. S. Regs., Part II. and the Staff Manual respectively. Title pages will be prepared in manuscript.

WAR DIARY or INTELLIGENCE SUMMARY.

(Erase heading not required.)

Army Form C. 2118.

2

Place	Date	Hour	Summary of Events and Information	Remarks and references to Appendices
ARMENTIERES	7/10/18		2nd LT PUGH was ordered to make a reconnaissance to A Co during the evening & is since reported missing. B Co comes back into Support line. casualties 1. OR Killed 4 OR wounded	
"	8/10/18		Enemy Shelling Battn heavily with Gas Shells. 52 casualties practically all B Co.	
"	9/10/18		The Battn was relieved by 11th CAMERONS. during relief enemy shelled Battn HQ and roads in the vicinity. CAPT. GROVES D.S.O. M.C. (2nd in command) was wounded in right forearm. 1 O.R also wounded. Transport Officer had his horse wounded and successfully delivered the rations under great difficulties.	APPENDIX 3
ERQUINGHEM	10/10/18		LT. GYE joins the Battn. The Battn now in Reserve at ERQUINGHEM. good billets. Draft of 60 men from England arrives and is posted to B Co. this Company having suffered heavy casualties	

A6945 Wt. W11422/M1160 350,000 12/16 D. D. & L. Forms/C./2118/14.

Volume No 5

15th Battn. K.O.Y.L.I.

October 1918

Instructions regarding War Diaries and Intelligence Summaries are contained in F. S. Regs., Part II. and the Staff Manual respectively. Title pages will be prepared in manuscript.

WAR DIARY
or
INTELLIGENCE SUMMARY.
(Erase heading not required.)

Army Form C. 2118.

3

Place	Date	Hour	Summary of Events and Information	Remarks and references to Appendices
ERQUINGHEM	11/10/18		Battn in reserve. Men cleaning up. C.O. inspects the new draft. B Co ordered to Support line to relieve one Company of 10th K.O.S.B. Raining hard during the day.	
	12/10/18		Relieved by the 23rd CHESHIRE REGT at noon. On relief the Battn moved back to DIV Support area East of STEENWERCK	APPENDIX 4
E of STEENWERCK	13/10/18		Men busy repairing huts in the camp. Baths allotted to Companies	
	14/10/18		The C.O. inspects Camp with regard to improvements. Rifle Range selected	
	15/10/18		Training during morning. Weather very bad, rain & cold.	
	16/10/18		During the morning orders come through to prepare to move at once, this being due to the enemy retiring. March off at 2pm to Rue Marle (South of ARMENTIERES) where the Battn is billetted for the night.	
RUE MARLE	17/10/18		March off at 9 am. The enemy having blown huge craters at all tactical points of roads made the journey-	

A6945 Wt. W11422/M1160 350,000 12/16 D. D. & L. Forms/C./2118/14.

Volume No 5

15th Battn.
K.O.Y.L.I.

October 1918

WAR DIARY
or
INTELLIGENCE SUMMARY.
(Erase heading not required.)

Army Form C. 2118.

Instructions regarding War Diaries and Intelligence Summaries are contained in F. S. Regs., Part II. and the Staff Manual respectively. Title pages will be prepared in manuscript.

Place	Date	Hour	Summary of Events and Information	Remarks and references to Appendices
RUE MARLE	17/10/18	Contd	particularly for the Battn Transport, very difficult. At midday the Battn rested for two hours and had dinner. About 4pm arrive at CHAMPREUILLE where the Battn is billetted for the night.	
CHAMPREUILLE	18/10/18		March off at 9am to WAMBRECHIES, on the line of march meet many French civilians who have been in the hands of the enemy since 1914. They were overjoyed to see British soldiers again. At noon while waiting for billets to be allotted the men have their dinners - good billets for all the Battn - later in the day the Companies find working parties to fill in the craters. BRIG GEN THE HON W.P. HORE RUTHVEN C.M.G. DSO. takes over command of the Brigade. BRIG GEN C.J. HOBKIRK CMG DSO being granted six months rest in England. The new Brigadier compliments the Battn on the	

Volume No 5

15th Battn
K. O. Y. L. I.

WAR DIARY
or
INTELLIGENCE SUMMARY.
(*Erase heading not required.*)

October 1918

Army Form C. 2118.

5

Instructions regarding War Diaries and Intelligence Summaries are contained in F. S. Regs., Part II. and the Staff Manual respectively. Title pages will be prepared in manuscript.

Place	Date	Hour	Summary of Events and Information	Remarks and references to Appendices
WAMBRECHIES	18/10/18	Contd	work of filling in the craters	
"	19/10/18		March off at 10 am to ST. ANDRE arriving about noon	
			The whole Brigade is billeted in a Monastery	
			every man having a bed. The C O inspects the	
			Billets immediately after arrival	
ST. ANDRE	20/10/18		The Division is now out of the line for a short period	APPENDIX 5
			to rest also to do the necessary work to improve	
			communications. The whole Battn working on	
			Railway in the afternoon.	
"	21/10/18		C O inspected Billets. Two Companies training	
			in the morning and working on Railway during the afternoon	
			The other two Companies working in the morning and	
			training in the afternoon.	
"	22/10/18		The Battn working during morning and training in the	
			afternoon. Weather exceptionally good at present.	

A6945 Wt. W11422/M1160 350,000 12/16 D. D. & L. Forms/C./2118/14.

Volume No 5

15th Battn. K.O.Y.L.I.

October 1918

Army Form C. 2118.

6

Instructions regarding War Diaries and Intelligence Summaries are contained in F. S. Regs., Part II. and the Staff Manual respectively. Title pages will be prepared in manuscript.

WAR DIARY
or
INTELLIGENCE SUMMARY.
(Erase heading not required.)

Place	Date	Hour	Summary of Events and Information	Remarks and references to Appendices
ST. ANDRE 23/10/18	23/9/18		All companies working during the morning and training in the afternoon.	
"	24/9/18		Two companies working during the morning and training in the afternoon, the other two companies training during the morning and working in the afternoon. Draft of 50 OR joined from base	
"	25/9/18		The Battn working on Railway all the morning. CO inspects the draft. CAPT A LINDEMERE proceeds to 231 RE Field Coy. to be attached for duty. Battalion Dinner was held attended by all Officers of the Battn. The following guests were entertained:- BRIG-GEN THE HON HORE RUTHVEN CMG DSO, CAPT T KNOX-SHAW M.C, CAPT. GLENDENNING R.E. CAPT THOMLINSON 10th K.O.S.B.	
"	26/9/18		Working Parties. One O.R. wounded while blowing up a wrecked bridge.	

A6945 Wt. W11422/M1160 350,000 12/16 D. D. & L. Forms/C./2118/14.

Volume No 5

15th Battn. K.O.Y.L.I.

WAR DIARY
or
INTELLIGENCE SUMMARY.
(*Erase heading not required.*)

October 1918

Army Form C. 2118.

7

Instructions regarding War Diaries and Intelligence Summaries are contained in F. S. Regs., Part II. and the Staff Manual respectively. Title pages will be prepared in manuscript.

Place	Date	Hour	Summary of Events and Information	Remarks and references to Appendices
ST ANDRE	27/9/18		Working Parties. 2nd LT ASHTON and 12 O.R proceed to base for re-classification of medical category.	
LANNOY	28/9/18		March to LANNOY arrive at midday. Brigadier compliments the Battn upon the good marching of the 11 miles. CO inspects billets immediately after arrival.	APPENDIX 6
"	29/9/18		LT COL T.W.T ISAAC leaves the Battn to attend Lewis Gun course for 7 days. CAPT T L WEBB takes over command of the Battn. All Companies training 9AM to 1pm	APPENDIX 7
"	30/9/18		Training during morning. In the afternoon football matches A Co v B Co and D Co v HQ	
"	31/9/18		Training 9AM to 1pm. No football weather too bad	
	1-11-18.		MWM Captain, Commanding 15th Bn K.O.Y.L.I.	

A6945 Wt. W11422/M1160 350,000 12/16 D. D. & L. Forms/C./2118/14.

Appendix I

SECRET. COPY NO.

15th Battalion, King's Own Yorkshire Light Infantry.

OPERATION ORDER No. [illegible].

by

MAJOR L. H. SANDISON, Commanding.

In the Field. 1st Oct. 1918

Ref. Map (1) The 15th Bn. K.O.Y.L.I. will relieve the 23rd Cheshire
1/20,000 Regt. in the front line to-night.
28 N.W. "B" Co. K.O.Y.L.I. will relieve "B" Co. Cheshires, Right front.

"C" " " " " "A" " Cheshires Left front

"A" " " " " "C" " Cheshires Right Support

"D" " " " " "D" " Cheshires Left Support.

Companies will march off independently in the following order:- "B" "C" "A" "D" Battalion H.Q. "B" Co. marching off at 6-30 p.m. Five minutes interval between Companies: 3 minutes interval between platoons after passing through [illegible].

ROUTE:- A.11.c.[illegible]: A.11.d.[illegible]: A.17.a.9.6.: A.17.d.1.3.: B.13.c.2.1, across country to OWL FARM, where one guide per platoon and one per Co. H.Q. will be in waiting at 1945.

DRESS:- Steel Helmets and S.B.Rs at the "Alert". Great coats to be carried on the back. Waterbottles to be filled before marching off.

(2) MAPS, ETC.

All maps, photographs, Defence Orders, etc., will be taken over and receipts forwarded to Bn. H.Q. as soon as possible after relief.

Companies will forward to Bn. H.Q. by 12 noon 2nd inst., sketch maps showing dispositions down to platoons

(3) Lewis Gun Limbers will follow Companies, and each limber will dump 2 boxes of S.A.A. at Bn. H.Q.

The number of Lewis Guns to be taken into the line has already been detailed.

(4) STORES. The following will be dumped at Company dumps near road immediately for transport to Q.M. Stores:-

Packs: Officers' valises: Co. Mess Boxes: Blankets in bundles of 10, and all surplus Co. Stores

(5) COOKS. Cookers will proceed to new Transport Lines after tea to-day.

(6) RATIONS. Rations to-night will be carried on the man. Pack mules will call at Co. H.Q. at 2345 with hot Soup in containers. These containers must be returned to [illegible] to-night.

(7) LOCATIONS.

Battalion H.Q. B.22.a.3.6.
Transport Lines }
Q.M. Stores } [illegible] CROSS, A.[illegible].9.
Bde. H.Q. (after 12 [illegible]), (2nd TOUQUET PARMENTIER.
Regtl. Aid Post. ~~[illegible]~~ To be notified later.
Cemetery. LE GRAND BEAUMART.

(8) ACKNOWLEDGE.

(Signed) J.W.[illegible].
Capt & A/Adjt.,
15th Bn., K.O.Y.L.I.

Copies to:-
1. C.O.
2. Adjt.
3. File
4-7 "A" - "D" Companies.
8. War Diary.
9. T.O.
10. Q.M.
11. R.S.M.
12. M.O.
13. 1[illegible]th Inf. Bde.

SECRET

Appendix II Copy No ....

Order No 21
by
Lt. Col. T.W.T. ISAAC,
Commanding 15th Battalion King's Own Yorkshire Light Infantry.

5-10-18.

Ref. Maps 1/20000 36 N.W.

1. The Battalion will relieve the 13th East Lancs. (119th Bde.) in the support area today.
   Order of March. Companies will march off independently in the following order - D, C, A, B, Headquarters, with 200 yds. between Cos. and 50 yds. between platoons.
   Starting Point. "D" Co. will pass the starting point at B.18.a.6.4 at 1845.
   Route. B.23.a.9.4 - B.18.a.6.4 - C.7.c.9.3, where one guide per Co. of the Innishillings will be in waiting to conduct Bn. to Pontoon Bridge at C.20.d.9.0. Here 1 guide per Co. will conduct Bn. to Bn. H.Q., where platoon guides will be provided.

2. Dispositions. The Bn. will be disposed as follows :-

   "A" Co. relieves "A" Co. E. Lanes.
   "B" " " "D" "
   "C" " " "C" " "
   "D" " " "B" "
   Bn. H.Q. C.22.c.2.6.

3. Lewis Gun Limbers will report to Co. H.Q. at 1630 and will follow Coss.

4. Transport. (a) Cookers will return to Transport Lines immediately.
   (b) 2 Limbers will report to Bn. H.Q. immediately. The Lewis Gun Reserve of 20 boxes, now at Bn. H.Q., will be dumped at new Bn. H.Q. & Bn. S.A.A. Reserve will also be at new Bn. H.Q.

5. Rations. Rations today will be carried up on the man. Water, fuel etc. will be carried up on the L.G. Limbers.

6. Canteen. O.C Details will arrange for canteen goods to be removed.

7. Trench Stores. Lists of Trench Stores will be sent to Bn. H.Q. as soon as possible after relief.

8. Winter Time. Winter Time will come into use tonight 5/6th inst. At 0100 hours (1 a.m. summer time) on 6th Oct., the clocks will be put back one hour. For purposes of Field and Signal Messages time will run on to 2459 hours on 5th October, and will then change to 0001 hours on 6th October.

9. Locations.

   Bn. H.Q. C.22.c.2.6. R.A.P. C.29.b.60.75.
   Bde. H.Q. TOUQUET-PARMENTIER, till 1000 on 7th inst.
   Transport Lines and Q.M. Stores - OWL FARM.

(Signed) J.W. Swanson, Capt. & A/Adjt.
15th K.O.Y.L.I.

Adyt

SECRET: Appendix III Copy No. ......

Operation Order No. 22
by
Lt. Col. T.W.T. ISAAC.
Commanding "Nth" Battalion, King's Own Yorkshire Light Infantry.
9-10-18.

Ref. Maps 1/20000 36 N.W.2.

1. The Bn. will be relieved tonight by the 11th CAMERONS and be withdrawn to Brigade Reserve in the ERQUINGHEM Area.

2. Inter-Battalion Relief.

"A" Co.	CAMERONS	relieves	"A" Co.	K.O.Y.L.I.
"B"	"	"	"C"	"
"C"	"	"	"B"	"
"D"	"	"	"D"	"

3. Guides. Two guides from each Co. will report to R.S.M. at Bn. H.Q. at 5 p.m.

4. All Trench Stores will be handed over, receipts obtained and forwarded to Bn. H.Q.

5. Completion of Relief of Cos. will be wired to Bn. H.Q. by code word "WHISKY."

6. Route. H.Qrs and "A", "B", "C" Cos. via Bn. H.Q. to junction of Main Road and Railway at C.27.a.2.1., thence along Railway running S.W. and W. to H.6.a.05.90. - Road to ERQUINGHEM. O.C. "D" Co. will choose his own route.

7. Transport. L.G. Limbers and H.Q. Limbers will meet Cos. at Bn. H.Q. at 10 p.m., and move off under T.O. Commanding Officer's horse to be at Pontoon Bridge C.20.d. at 10 p.m.

8. The Q.M. will arrange for hot tea when Cos. arrive at billets and for C.Q.M. Sgts. to meet Cos. at H.4.d.2.6. at midnight.

9. Certificates that all men are in billets, and fire and gas precautions taken, to be rendered by Co. Commanders on arrival at billets.

10. Feet. Feet will be washed and rubbed with whale-oil tomorrow morning, and socks changed. Q.M. will arrange. Certificates that feet of all men in respective Cos. have been inspected by an officer will be rendered by Co. Commanders. 2nd Lieut. JOLLEY will arrange for H.Q.

11. ACKNOWLEDGE.

(Signed) J.W. Swanson,
Capt. & A./Adjt.
"Nth" Bn., K.O.Y.L.I.

Copies to :-

1. Brigade
2. C.O.
3. Q.M.
4. T.O.
5. O.C. "A" Co.
6. O.C. "B" Co.
7. O.C. "C" Co.
8. O.C. "D" Co.
9. Cameron Hrs.
10. War Diary.
11. File.
12. M.O.

SECRET. Appendix IV COPY NO. 4

15th Battalion, King's Own Yorkshire Light Infantry
ORDER NO. 23.
by
LIEUT.COLONEL T.H.T.ISAAC, Commanding.

In the Field. 13-1-18.

Ref.Map. 36 N.W.(2) 1/20,000

(1) The Battalion will be relieved to-morrow by the 23rd Bn. CHESHIRE REGT., and will be withdrawn to Divisional Support in the NIPPON BEND Area.

(2) The Battalion will move off as follows:-
"D" Co., "C" Co., "A" Co., "B" Co., Bn. H.Q.
"D" Co. passing the Starting Point at 1400.
15 minutes interval between Companies.
Starting Point:- PONTOON BRIDGE. - B.4.c.
Route:- PONTOON BRIDGE - ORVILLE JUNCTION - OWL FARM - Cross country to B.15.d.9.0. where C.Q.M.Sgts. will be in waiting at 1430 to guide in Companies.

(3) ADVANCE PARTY. This has been detailed separately.

(4) TRANSPORT.
Lewis Gun Limbers, and one other limber will report to Companies at 1230.
(a) Packs. - will be carried on Co. limbers.
(b) Officers' Valises. A G.S. wagon will call at Co. H.Q. and Bn. H.Q. for Officers' valises, commencing with Bn.H.Q. at 1200.
(c) Regimental Transport. - will move off under the Transport Officer at 1330.
(d) Co. Commanders' horses will be at Co. H.Q. at 1300.

(5) BLANKETS.
Q.M. will arrange for blankets to be dumped at new camp by 1600.

(6) CERTIFICATES.
Certificates that all men are in billets, and fire and gas precautions taken, to be rendered by Co. Commanders after arrival at billets.

(7) LOCATIONS.

Bn. H.Q.	B.19.a.2.3.
Transport Lines & Q.M. Stores ..	OWL FARM.
Regtl. Aid Post....	Bn. H.Q.
Bde. H.Q.	TOUQUET PARMENTIER. (after 1000 on 14th)

(8) ACKNOWLEDGE.

(Signed) J.W.SWANSON,
Capt. & Adjutant,
15th Battalion K.O.Y.L.I.

COPIES TO:-
1. C.O.
2. Adjt.
3. File.
4. War Diary.
5. Q.M.
6. T.O.
7. Sig. Officer.
8 - 11 "A" - "D" Cos.
12. R.S.M.
13. 120th Bde.
14. 23rd Cheshire Regt.

Appendix V

SPECIAL ORDER OF THE DAY

- by -

MAJOR-GENERAL SIR W.E. PEYTON, K.C.B., K.C.V.O., D.S.O.,

COMMANDING 40TH DIVISION.

Headquarters, 40th Division.
19th October, 1918.

After three months most strenuous work in the Line the 40th Division is being temporarily withdrawn. The Divisional Commander would like to take this opportunity of expressing to all ranks his appreciation of and his gratitude for their soldier like attitude under trying and arduous conditions. Much has been asked of the endurance and courage of all ranks and it has at all times been met with admirable response. Such pressure has been brought on the enemy that his flight has been unexpectedly rapid. Roads, railways and bridges have been destroyed and before a further organized advance can be undertaken these important communications must be restored. The task of the Division for a short period will be to do its utmost to restore these communications as rapidly as possible and the Divisional Commander calls upon all ranks to put all their energy into this work so that the glorious advance to final victory may be completed. Training during this period must not be neglected for if any efforts of the Divisional Commander can ensure it, the 40th Division will be in at the death.

C.G. Moore

Lieut.-Colonel,
A.A. & Q.M.G.,

Appendix VI

SECRET

Copy No. 3.....

15th Battalion K. O. Y. L. I.

27-10-1918.
[illegible]

MARCH ORDER NO. 1.

Ref, Maps 1/40,000 Sheets 36 & 37.

(1) The battalion will move to LANNOY to-morrow.

(2) ORDER OF MARCH. Starting point - H.34.a.7.0.

Companies will parade facing South on road opposite Brigade Headquarters at 0815 in the following order :-

Bn. H.Q. "A" "B" "C" "D" Companies.

(3) DRESS. Marching order. S.B.Rs. slung. Steel Helmets to be carried on the left shoulder strap. Water Bottles to be filledbefore marching off.

Captain Webb will act as Second in Command and will ride in rear of the Battalion. One Subaltern and two N.C.Os. to be detailed by O/C "A" Coy will march in rear of Battalion acting as rear party to collect stragglers.

(4) OFFICERS CHARGERS will be at Q.M. Stores at 0815.

ADMINISTRATIVE

(5) (a) BLANKETS In bundles of 10 and labelled.
(b) PACKS containing greatcoats
(c) JERKINS In bundles of 10
} To be dumped at yard in Transport Lines by 0700.

(B) OFFICERS VALISES to be at Q.M. Stores by 0730.

(C) COMPANY MESS BOX & STATIONERY BOX to be carried on Company Cooker and Company L.G. Limber.

(D) LOADING PARTY has been detailed separately.

(E) ADVANCE PARTY - 4 C.Q.M.Ss. will report to 2/Lieut. J.Williams at 0730.

TRANSPORT.

(6) LEWIS GUN LIMBERS will follow Companies. 8 pack mules will follow Battalion. Remaining transport will move under Brigade Transport Officer at 0841.

(7) ACKNOWLEDGE.

(Signed) J.W. SWANSON.
Captain and Adjutant.
15th Battalion K.O.Y.L.I.

Copies to :,
1. C.O.
2. Adjt
3. War Diary
4-7. A - D Coys
8. Q.M.
9. T.O.
10. I.O.
11. M.O.
12. R.S.M.
13. 106th Bde.

(To be rendered in triplicate for each man.)

Form A.G. 544/1 (M).

(*a*) Unit .... (*b*)* .... (*c*)* ....

RELEASE FROM THE ARMY FOR COAL-MINING (OVERSEAS).

PART "A."

No. .... Name .... Rank .... Medical Category† ....

Unit .... Corps .... Civil Occupation‡ ....

Name and address of Colliery firm with whom last employed previous to August, 1914 ....

Period of employment with such ....

Home address ....

Mine at which last worked ....

Physical disability (if any) preventing work at his trade† ....

I am willing to be transferred to Class "W" or W(P) of the Army Reserve for the above purpose.

I certify that the above particulars are a true statement of fact.

Date ....

Signature of applicant.

The above particulars have been compared with the entries in Army Book 64, and I am of the opinion that the applicant was a coal-miner employed as such before August 4th, 1914.

....

Signature of O.C. Unit.

TO BE FORWARDED TO THE OFFICER COMMANDING LABOUR GROUP CONCERNED

NOTE:—These two spaces will be filled in as follows:—

* (*b*) First three letters (in Block Capitals) of name of mine referred to in 2.

* (*c*) Name of mine in full.

e.g. (*b*) AMB.

(*c*) Ambler Thorn.

† To be verified by O.C. Unit.

‡ Insert local term for precise colliery occupation at which you were employed.

PART "B."

To Deputy Adjutant General,

3rd Echelon, G.H.Q.

I have interviewed the above-mentioned man and consider that he fulfills the conditions for release laid down, and that he should be sent home for coal-mining purposes.

Date ....

Interviewing Official.

A duplicate of the form will be forwarded at this stage by the interviewing official to the Controller of Coal Mines, Room 427, Holborn Viaduct Hotel, London, E.C.1, the letters P.M.E. being clearly marked in the left-hand top corner of the envelope.

PRINTED IN FRANCE BY ARMY PRINTING AND STATIONERY SERVICES   PRESS A—9/18—7284S—100,000.

Appendix VII — File

BATTALION ORDERS
by
CAPTAIN T.L.WEBB
Commanding 15th Battalion King's Own Yorkshire Light Infantry.

LENNOY — 29-10-1918

DETAIL.

Orderly Officer tomorrow..... 2/Lieut. H.H.BAGDEN
Next for Duty................ " J.C.WATERTON
Company on Duty tomorrow..... "B" Company
Next for Duty................ "C" "

483. ROUTINE

Reveille...... 06.30
Sick Parade... 07.15
Breakfast..... 07.30
First Parade.. 08.30
Dinners....... 12.30
Tea........... 16.30
Lights Out.... 21.30

484. TRAINING

Coys.	08.30 - 0930	0930 - 1030	1045 - 1130	1130 - 1230
A	Gas & Steady Drill	PT & BF	Battle Formations	Battalion Scheme Battle Formations.
B	Steady Drill	Battle Formations	PT & BF	
C	PT & BF	Battle Formations	Gas & Steady Drill	
D	Battle Formations	Gas & Steady Drill	Mushetry	

LOCATION - G.21.b

Companies will assemble near CHIMNEY STACK at 1130.

LEWIS GUNNERS, SIGNALLERS & STRETCHER BEARERS PARADE - As usual under respective specialist Officers.

SPECIALIST N.C.Os. report to Companies. Time & Place as above.

485. BOUNDS. The Bounds of the Brigade Billeting Area D are :-

Cross roads G.11.c.2.6. - Cross roads G.10.a.4.5. -
Cross roads G.8.b.8.6. - Railway crossing G.15.c.1.0.
Cross roads G.16.a.0.8.

486. DRESS.

No man will proceed beyond his Battalion Billeting Area unless he is properly dressed with belt and sidearms and small box respirator. Battalions will place notice boards around their areas as soon as possible.

487. COMMAND.

Captain T.L.WEBB will assume Command of 15th Battalion K.O.Y.L.I. during the temporary absence of Lieut,-Col. T.W.T.ISAAC on a Course.

(To be rendered in triplicate for each man.)

Form A.G. 544/1 (M).

(*a*) Unit .... (*b*)* .... (*c*)* ....

RELEASE FROM THE ARMY FOR COAL-MINING (OVERSEAS).

PART "A."

No. .... Name .... Rank .... Medical Category† ....

Unit .... Corps .... Civil Occupation‡ ....

Name and address of Colliery firm with whom last employed previous to August, 1914 ....

Period of employment with such ....

Home address ....

Mine at which last worked ....

Physical disability (if any) preventing work at his trade† ....

I am willing to be transferred to Class "W" or W(P) of the Army Reserve for the above purpose.

I certify that the above particulars are a true statement of fact.

Date ....

Signature of applicant.

The above particulars have been compared with the entries in Army Book 64, and I am of the opinion that the applicant was a coal-miner employed as such before August 4th, 1914.

....

Signature of O.C. Unit.

TO BE FORWARDED TO THE OFFICER COMMANDING LABOUR GROUP CONCERNED.

NOTE:—These two spaces will be filled in as follows:—

* (*b*) First three letters (in Block Capitals) of name of mine referred to in 2.
* (*c*) Name of mine in full.
e.g. (*b*) AMB.
(*c*) Ambler Thorn.

† To be verified by O.C. Unit.
‡ Insert local term for precise colliery occupation at which you were employed.

PART "B."

To Deputy Adjutant General,
3rd Echelon, G.H.Q.

I have interviewed the above-mentioned man and consider that he fulfills the conditions for release laid down, and that he should be sent home for coal-mining purposes.

Date ....

Interviewing Official.

A duplicate of the form will be forwarded at this stage by the interviewing official to the Controller of Coal Mines, Room 427, Holborn Viaduct Hotel, London, E.C.1, the letters P.M.E. being clearly marked in the left-hand top corner of the envelope.

PRINTED IN FRANCE BY ARMY PRINTING AND STATIONERY SERVICES.   PRESS A—9/18—7984S—100,000.

continued

458. LECTURE - VENEREAL DISEASE

The Battalion Medical Officer will lecture Companies on Venereal Disease tomorrow in "C" Company's billet as follows :-

"C" Company	-	1400	"A" Company	-	1430
"D" "	-	1415	"B" "	-	1445

All Officers & N.C.Os. except those on duty will attend.

(Signed) J.W.SWANSON Capt. & Adjt.
15th Battalion K.O.Y.L.I.

NOTICE

THE "GAMECOCKS"

The Gamecocks perform nightly at 1800 hours at LANNOY.

PART "C."

To The Secretary (Mob. 5d), War Office, Kew, London, S.W.1.

The above-mentioned soldier is suitable for release as a coal-miner and will be employed by .... at ....

Please arrange for his transfer to the Reserve and despatch to the address shown.

....

Date........................ *Signature*..
for Controller of Coal Mines.

PART "D."

To The O.C. Discharge Centre........................Command.

The above-mentioned soldier has been ordered to report to you on........................ for transfer to the Reserve for work in a coal mine.

The Deputy Adjutant General, 3rd Echelon, B.E.F., France, has been instructed to despatch to you A.F.s B.103 and 122 and the Officer i/c Records has been ordered to forward to you A.F. B.178 and 120.

The soldier will be transferred to the Reserve and despatched to the address shown in part "C" of this form.

Date........................ ....
Signature, Director of Mobilization.

PART "E."

To..(firm).

....(address).

The soldier referred to in Part "A" of this form has been transferred to Class.............. of the Reserve.

He has been despatched to you to-day.

Please complete and forward Part "F" of this form as early as possible to the address shown therein.

If at any time the soldier in question should leave your employment, you should immediately report the fact to the Secretary, War Office, Mob. 5d, Kew, London, S.W.1, stating the reasons for which he left your employment.

Date........................ ....*Rank.*

Commanding

....*Discharge Centre.*

PART "F."

To The Secretary, War Office, Mob. 5*d*,
Kew, London, S.W. 1.

The soldier referred to in Part "A" of this form reported to me to-day.

Date........................ ....
(Signature, Colliery Firm.)

LE 3 OCTOBRE, 1918.

ARMEE BELGE.
Chef d' Etat-Major General.

Mon cher General,

Incertain de pouvoir truver le temps d'aller vous voir, je m'empresse de vous addresser mes plus chalsureuses felicitations pour les magnifiques success remportes par les troupes de la 11° Armee Britannque, dans l'offensive declenchee le 28 septembre dernier.

Votre habile direction et le merveilleux alan de vos combattantes n'ent pas seulement delivre de l'oppression ennemie une partie du territoire national, ils ont aussi permis a l'armme Belge de concourir avec success au même but; l'attaque conjugee realisee victorieusement en cette occasion par le second corps, l'a aides dans la perfection. Je tiens a vous en exprimer ainsi qu'au general Sir Jacob ma plus vive gratitude.

En outre de ce soutien, la 11° Armee Britannique a prete efficacement a nos operations le concours direct d'une partie de son artillerie et de son aviation.

Cette dernier tout particulierement a fait preuve, en depit de circonstances atmo spheriques des plus defavourables, de qualities combattives si elevees que notre Armee gardera toujours le souvenir vivace des exploits glorieux et feconds dont elle a ete le temoin ces derniers jours.

Je serais vraiment heureux, Mon Cher General, si vous vouliez bien faire part de mon admiration, de ma reconnaissance et de mes felicitations a la belle 11° Armee sous votre commandement et tout principalement a l'Aviation et a l'Artillerie qui ont secondes directement nos operations.

Veuillez, Mon Cher General, agreer l'expression de mes sentiments les meilleurs.

(Sgd) G I L L A I N.

A Monsieur le Lieutenant General Plumer,
Commandant la Second Armee Brittanique.

- 2 -

Headquarters, Second Army.

My dear General,

On behalf of the troops of the Second Army I beg to thank you very warmly for the tribute paid to them in your letter of to-day.

The contents of your letter will be communicated to all the troops concerned.

Allow me to offer to you and through you to all the troops of the Belgian Army my personal congratulations on the splendid success achieved by them and to day on behalf on the Second Army how proud we all are to have co-operated with them.

Believe me,
Yours sincerely,

(Sgd) Herbert Plumer.

Warstory

120th Inf. Bde. No. 120/429.

HEADQUARTERS, 120th INFANTRY BRIGADE.

Appendix VIII

10th Bn. K.O.S.B.
15th Bn. K.O.Y.L.I.
11th Bn. Cam. Highrs.
120th T. M. Battery.

The attached copy of letter from General GILLAIN, Chief of the General Staff, Belgian Army, and the Army Commander'sreply thereto, os forwarded for your information and communication to all ranks.

T Keenshaw
for Captain,
Brigade Major,
120th Infan ry Brigade.

8-10-18.

6A

VR 6

CONFIDENTIAL

WAR DIARY

of

15th Battalion K.O.Y.L.I.

for the month

of

NOVEMBER 1918

VOLUME No. VI

SECRET

[illegible]
Lieut: Colonel
Commanding 15th Bn K.O.Y.L.I.

Volume VI

15th Bn K.O.Y.L.I.
November 1918

WAR DIARY
or
INTELLIGENCE SUMMARY.
(*Erase heading not required.*)

Army Form C. 2118.

Page 1

Instructions regarding War Diaries and Intelligence Summaries are contained in F. S. Regs., Part II. and the Staff Manual respectively. Title pages will be prepared in manuscript.

Place	Date	Hour	Summary of Events and Information	Remarks and references to Appendices
LANNOY	1/11/18		Batt Training - Brigadier saw Battn carrying out practice Battle formations - Inter Company Football matches in the afternoon - News received of Armistice signed with Austria.	APPENDIX I
				KV
	2/11/18		Batt Training - Football matches in the afternoon.	KV
	3/11/18		Divine Service.	KV
	4/11/18		Rifle Competition at Rifle Range at COHEM - ~~...~~ the best aggregate score being obtained by SGT LEASON.	APPENDIX II
			Brigadier saw Officers of the Battn doing Outpost scheme during the afternoon.	KV
	5/11/18		Rained all day. training in Billets	
	6/11/18		Move to NECHIN - Billets good but men rather crowded	APPENDIX III
			Battn now in Div Support.	KV
NECHIN	7/11/18		Training - A Co carry out scheme - Company in attack	KV
	8/11/18		Training - B C + D Cos practise Company in attack.	KV
	9/11/18		2nd LT F.T. THEWLIS awarded military cross for	APPENDIX IV

A6945 Wt. W11422/M1160 350,000 12/16 D. D. & L. Forms/C./2118/14.

Volume VI

Instructions regarding War Diaries and Intelligence Summaries are contained in F. S. Regs., Part II. and the Staff Manual respectively. Title pages will be prepared in manuscript.

15th Bn K.O.Y.L.I.
November 1918.

WAR DIARY
or
INTELLIGENCE SUMMARY.
(Erase heading not required.)

Army Form C. 2118.

Page 11

Place	Date	Hour	Summary of Events and Information	Remarks and references to Appendices
NECHIN	9/11/18		"Conspicuous Gallantry & devotion to duty while acting as Transport Officer" Training as usual.	
	[illegible]		LT COL ISAAC returns from course and again assumes command of the Battn vice CAPT. T.L. WEBB	
			Move to PECQ which was found to be much devastated. Battn billeted in empty houses.	APPENDIX V
HERINNES	10/11/18		Move across River SCHELDT to HERINNES. Battn billeted in farm buildings which made good billets for troops.	
	11/11/18		At 6.45 am signallers received unofficial news that Armistice had been signed, this was confirmed at 9.50 AM. CAPT T.L. WEBB procured 1000 pkts of cigarettes & 700 packets of toffee for the troops. These were distributed in the evening when the Companies were holding a sing song to celebrate the Armistice	APPENDIX VI

Volume VI

15th Bn K.O.Y.L.I.
November 1918

Army Form C. 2118.

WAR DIARY
or
INTELLIGENCE SUMMARY.
(Erase heading not required.)

Instructions regarding War Diaries and Intelligence Summaries are contained in F. S. Regs., Part II. and the Staff Manual respectively. Title pages will be prepared in manuscript.

Page VII

Place	Date	Hour	Summary of Events and Information	Remarks and references to Appendices
HERRINNES	12/11/18		Battn moved back to Billets at BUCQUOI. B & C Cos billeted in convent, A Co in farms and D Co in Houses all comfortable.	APPENDIX VII
BUCQUOI	13/11/18		Training – CO's parade at 10.30 AM. Draft of 4 NCO's & 65 OR arrive from Base.	APPENDIX VIII
	14/11/18		CO's parade at 9.30 am. CO & Padre attend Conference on Educational Scheme.	
	15/11/18		Training – Brigade Ceremonial parade at 10.30 am. It was arranged to hold Bn sports on the next day	APPENDIX IX
	16/11/18		Training – Route March 9.30 am. Bn Sports held in the afternoon. The G.O.C's Division & Brigade also General Crozier G.O.C. 119 Brigade were present. Divisional Band was in attendance. Afternoon fine though cold. Some excellent running was witnessed. The following officers appeared in the Supplement to the London Gazette dated 13th as appointed to the Bn Major H.J.R. Beck, Capt A Lindemere, L.M. Sandison, G.N. Watney, T.L. Webb Lts. W.R. Pearson & R.S. Walton 2nd Lts	APPENDIX X APPENDIX XI

A6945 Wt. W11422/M1160 350,000 12/16 D. D. & L. Forms/C./2118/14.

Volume VI

15th Bn K.O.Y.L.I.
November 1918.

WAR DIARY
or
INTELLIGENCE SUMMARY.
(Erase heading not required.)

Army Form C. 2118.

Instructions regarding War Diaries and Intelligence Summaries are contained in F. S. Regs., Part II. and the Staff Manual respectively. Title pages will be prepared in manuscript.

Page iv

Place	Date	Hour	Summary of Events and Information	Remarks and references to Appendices
BUCQUOI	16/11/18	(Cont)	2nd Lts G. Blewitt G.F. Beeching C.P. Prest J.W. Swanson F.L. Blagden H.E. Basden G.L.R. Brown. B.O. Denham. F.W.W. Dron	
			The following extract appeared in Supplement to London Gazette dated 14/11/18 Capt L.M. Sandison to be Temp Major (June 11) Temp 2nd Lts to be Temp Capts J.W. Swanson (June 11) A Morrow (att a) (Aug 2)	
			The following appointment was made. T/Capt. T.L. Webb to be acting Major with effect from 24/10/18 while acting as Second-in-Command.	~~APPENDIX XI~~
	17/11/18		Army thanksgiving service held at Roubaix. 95 O.R.s taken from the 3 Bns in Brigade under Command of Major T.L. Webb attended. divine service followed by March past. F.M. Sir Douglas Haigh.	
			Divisional thanksgiving service held in "Gamecocks" Salle Sammy 10 am	
	18/11/18		Training - Brigade Ceremonial parade on parade ground at Nechin. Divisional Band in attendance. G.O.C. Division present.	APPENDIX XII
	19/11/18		Brigade inspected by the Corps Commander at Nechin at 11.00.	APPENDIX XIII
	20/11/18		Training - under Company Commanders. The following extract taken from Supplement to London Gazette dated 8th Oct 1918. Major T.W.T. Isaac to be Temp Lieut Colonel (16th Apr 1918)	APPENDIX XIV

D. D. & L., London, E.C.
(10340) Wt W5300/P713 750,000 3/18 Sch. 2688 Forms/C2118/15.

Volume VI

15th Bn. K.O.Y.L.I.
November 1918

WAR DIARY
or
INTELLIGENCE SUMMARY.
(Erase heading not required.)

Army Form C. 2118.

Instructions regarding War Diaries and Intelligence Summaries are contained in F. S. Regs., Part II. and the Staff Manual respectively. Title pages will be prepared in manuscript.

Page V

Place	Date	Hour	Summary of Events and Information	Remarks and references to Appendices
BUCQUOI	21/11/18		Training under Company Commanders. Lectures by Capt. D McL Oman on Demobilization to C & D Coys	KV
	22/11/18		Training under Company Commanders. Major T L Webb assumed command of the Bn during absence of Lt Col T.W.T. Isaacs to command of 120th Brigade. Lectures as above by Capt Oman to A & B Coys. Personel of the 120th Bde TMB rejoined the Battalion. Football A & B Coy v C & D Coy.	KV
	23/11/18		Training. Bn Ceremonial parade at Nechin. Lewis guns on parade	KV
	24/11/18		Devine Service 10.00. Football in afternoon A & B Coy v D Coy. No 64092 Cpl (L/Sgt) R W Shaw awarded the Military Medal for gallantry in action and Devotion to duty	APPENDIX XV KD
	25/11/18		Training under Company Commanders. Educational classes commenced. Recreation room opened. Lt Col T.W.T. Isaac assumed command of the battalion	KV
	26/11/18		Training under Company Commanders. Bde H.Q. move to Launoy & B Coy take over Bde Billets. 4 Officers from the Cameron Highlanders attached to us for duty. G.O.C inspected A Company.	APPENDIX XVI KV
	28/11/18		Training under Company Cmdrs. G.O.C inspected B Company. Football match against Cameron Highlanders. Result drawn game 2-2	

Lieut Cole
Commanding 15th Bn KOYLI

D. D. & L., London, E.C.
(10340) Wt W5300/P713 750,000 3/18 Sch. 2688 Forms/C2118/15.

APPENDIX I

BATTALION ORDERS
BY
CAPTAIN [illegible], COMMANDING
13th Battalion King's Own Yorkshire Light Infantry.

DETAIL

Orderly Officer for tomorrow.............. 2/Lieut.J.[illegible]otcherby
Next for duty................................ 2/Lieut.G.Brown
Company on duty tomorrow................. "D" Company
Next for Duty................................ "A" Company

647 ROUTINE

Reveille.................. 0630
Breakfast................. 0730
Sick Parade............... 0715
Dinners................... 1300
Orderly Room.............. 1230
Tea....................... 1600
Lights Out................ 2130

648 MEDICAL PARADE

There will be a Battalion Medical Parade tomorrow as follows - usual place :-

"A" Coy. 0730 "C" Coy. 0750
"B" " 0740 "D" " 0800

649 TRAINING

LEWIS GUNNERS, SIGNALLERS, STRETCHER BEARERS will parade as detailed under respective Specialist Instructors.

650 BOMBING

2/Lieut. G. Brown will act as Battalion Bombing Officer and will arrange direct with O's/C. Coys. and Quartermaster for supply of dummy and practice bombs.

651 TRAINING

Training Programme for 1st proximo.

Coy.	0830 to 0900	0900 to 0930	0930 to 1000	1000 to 1030	1030 to 1100	1100 to 1130	1130 to 1230
"A"	Coy. Commdrs Parade.	Gas Chamber	Bombing.		Extended Order		P.T. & B.F.
"B"	P.T. & B.F.	P.T. & B.F.	Musketry.	Gas Chamber	~~Musketry.~~ Bombing		Extended Order.
"C"	Bombing.		Extended Order.		P.T. & B.F.	Gas Chamber	Musketry 1140 - 1230
"D"	EXTENDED ORDER		P. T. & B.F.		Gas Chamber.	Musketry.	Bombing.

EXTENDED ORDER. The attention of Officers Commanding Companies is drawn to Infantry Training, Section [illegible] - para [illegible] for the correct method of extending in open order.

(To be rendered in triplicate for each man.)

Form A.G. 544/1 (M).

(*a*) Unit .... (*b*)* .... (*c*)* ....

RELEASE FROM THE ARMY FOR COAL-MINING (OVERSEAS).

PART "A."

No. .... Name .... Rank .... Medical Category† ....

Unit .... Corps .... Civil Occupation‡ ....

Name and address of Colliery firm with whom last employed previous to August, 1914 ....

Period of employment with such ....

Home address ....

Mine at which last worked ....

Physical disability (if any) preventing work at his trade† ....

I am willing to be transferred to Class "W" or W(P) of the Army Reserve for the above purpose.

I certify that the above particulars are a true statement of fact.

Date ....

Signature of applicant.

The above particulars have been compared with the entries in Army Book 64, and I am of the opinion that the applicant was a coal-miner employed as such before August 4th, 1914.

....

Signature of O.C. Unit.

TO BE FORWARDED TO THE OFFICER COMMANDING LABOUR GROUP CONCERNED.

NOTE:—These two spaces will be filled in as follows:—

* (*b*) First three letters (in Block Capitals) of name of mine referred to in 2.

* (*c*) Name of mine in full.

e.g. (*b*) AMB.

(*c*) Ambler Thorn.

† To be verified by O.C. Unit.

‡ Insert local term for precise colliery occupation at which you were employed.

PART "B."

To Deputy Adjutant General,

3rd Echelon, G.H.Q.

I have interviewed the above-mentioned man and consider that he fulfills the conditions for release laid down, and that he should be sent home for coal-mining purposes.

Date ....

Interviewing Official.

A duplicate of the form will be forwarded at this stage by the interviewing official to the Controller of Coal Mines, Room 427, Holborn Viaduct Hotel, London, E.C.1, the letters P.M.E. being clearly marked in the left-hand top corner of the envelope.

PRINTED IN FRANCE BY ARMY PRINTING AND STATIONERY SERVICES. PRESS A—9/18—7984S—100,000.

652 GAS CHAMBER

The Gas Chamber, near Brigade Headquarters, is allotted to Companies tomorrow as follows :-

"A" Company..............0900 - 0930
Bn. H.Q. & Transport....0930 - 1000
"B" Company..............1000 - 1030
"D" Company..............1030 - 1100
"C" Company..............1115 - 1145

O/C Coys and R.S.M. will ensure that all servants, orderlies etc. parade withntheir Coys.

The Battn. Gas N.C.O. will arrange to meet Coys. at Brig'de H.Q. to guide them to Gas Chamber.

653 ALARM POST

In the event of an alarm, Coys. will fall in on the Square.

Dress - Fighting Order.
Packs and blanketsand Officers Valises will be dumped in present quarters.
Lewis Gun Limbers ill be loaded.
Further Orders will then be isued.
All ranks are to be acquianted with these Orders.

654 POSTINGS - INTER COMPANY

The following cross postings will take effect from today.

No. 330742	Pte.	Sadler	"A"	Coy posted to		"B"	Coy
64103	"	Evans E.T	A	"	...	"C"	"
64769	"	Watton J.	"D"	"	...	"C"	"
64740	"	Smith WHP	"D"	"	...	"C"	"
64725	"	Pattinson	"D"	"	...	"C"	"
64633	"	Carroll J.	D"	"	...	"C"	"

PART 11

APPOINTMENTS & PROMOTIONS

No. 64178 Sergt. W.A.A.Evans "A" Coy. appointed A/C.S.M. (paid) 18-10-1918 (vice No. 65001 C.S.M. Charlwood A. to United Kingdom as Cadet).

Assumes duties 16-10-1918

No238068 Sergt, S,Harrison "A" Company appointed A/C.Q.M.S. (paid) 7-9-1918 (vice No. 64187 C.Q.M.S. Bond C.A. to United Kingdom).

Assumes duties 7-9-1918.

LANNOY
31-10-1918

(signed) J.W.SWANSON Capt
Adjutant, 15th Battalion K.O.Y.L.I.

NOTICE

An armistice was signed with Turkey, and takes effect from noon to-day.

ITALIAN FRONT The advance is continuing rapidly. The Italian Troops have captured VITTORIA, and the British Troops have entered ASIAGO. 50,000 prisoners have been taken and the Austrian Army is reported disorganized, and cut in half by LORD CAVAN'S Army.

(To be rendered in triplicate for each man.)

Form A.G. 544/1 (M).

(a) Unit .... (b)* .... (c)* ....

RELEASE FROM THE ARMY FOR COAL-MINING (OVERSEAS).

PART "A."

No. .... Name .... Rank .... Medical Category† ....

Unit .... Corps .... Civil Occupation‡ ....

Name and address of Colliery firm with whom last employed previous to August, 1914 ....

Period of employment with such ....

Home address ....

Mine at which last worked ....

Physical disability (if any) preventing work at his trade† ....

I am willing to be transferred to Class "W" or W(P) of the Army Reserve for the above purpose.

I certify that the above particulars are a true statement of fact.

Date ....

Signature of applicant.

The above particulars have been compared with the entries in Army Book 64, and I am of the opinion that the applicant was a coal-miner employed as such before August 4th, 1914.

....

Signature of O.C. Unit.

TO BE FORWARDED TO THE OFFICER COMMANDING LABOUR GROUP CONCERNED.

NOTE:—These two spaces will be filled in as follows:—

* (b) First three letters (in Block Capitals) of name of mine referred to in 2.

* (c) Name of mine in full.

e.g. (b) AMB.

(c) Ambler Thorn.

† To be verified by O.C. Unit.

‡ Insert local term for precise colliery occupation at which you were employed.

PART "B."

To Deputy Adjutant General,

3rd Echelon, G.H.Q.

I have interviewed the above-mentioned man and consider that he fulfills the conditions for release laid down, and that he should be sent home for coal-mining purposes.

Date ....

Interviewing Official.

A duplicate of the form will be forwarded at this stage by the interviewing official to the Controller of Coal Mines, Room 427, Holborn Viaduct Hotel, London, E.C.1, the letters P.M.E. being clearly marked in the left-hand top corner of the envelope.

PRINTED IN FRANCE BY ARMY PRINTING AND STATIONERY SERVICES. PRESS A—9/18—79848—100,000.

APPENDIX II

15th Battalion King's Own Yorkshire Light Infantry.

RIFLE COMPETITION Nov. 4th 1918

Practice	Distance	No of Rounds	Conditions	Points			
				Bull	Inner	Mag.	Outer
Application 1.	100 Metres	5	Bayonet fixed. Standing with rest "9" Bull	4	3	2	1
Snap. 2.	100 Metres	5	Bayonet fixed Standing with rest. Silhouette target. 4 Secs. allowed.	3 Points for every hit			
Application 3.	100 Metres	5	Bayonet fixed Standing with rest. Gas Masks on. 9" Bull.	4	3	2	1
Rapid. 4.	100 Metres	15	Bayonet fixed. 9" Bull. Time 60 secs. 5 rds. in mag. remaining chargers from pouch.	4	3	2	1
Application 5.	300 Metres	5	Bayonet fixed, Lying, firing round cover. 18" Bull.	4	3	2	1
Rapid. 6.	300 Metres.	5	Bayonet fixed. Lying, firing round cover. 18" Bull, Mag. charged	4	3	2	1

RULES

Companies will forward to Orderly Room the names of N.C.Os. and men desirous of competing. Not less than 12 entries from each Company.
Entries to be in Orderly Room by Nov. 3rd.
Individual Scores for each Practice.
Prizes will be given as follows :-

	1st	2nd	3rd
Each Practice....................	10 Frs	5 Frs	---
Highest Aggregate................	40 Frs	20 Frs	10 Frs.

APPENDIX III

SECRET 15th. Battn. K.O.Y.L.I. Copy No..11...

MARCH ORDER NO. 2 5/11/1918

Ref Map Sheet 57 1/40.000

1. MOVE The Battalion will move to NECHIN tomorrow.

2. ORDER OF MARCH Starting point - The Square. Companies will parade outside present billets at 0915. Battalion H.Q. will clear the Square at 0920 followed by "A" "B" "C" and "D" Coys.
The intervals laid down in S.S. 724 will be maintained between Companies and vehicles.

3. DRESS Marching Order with packs. S.B.Rs. slung, Steel Helmets to be carried on the left shoulder strap. Water Bottles to be filled before marching off.

Captain F. Fisher will act as Second-in-Command and will ride in rear of the Battalion.

One subbaltern and two N.C.Os. to be detailed by O/C. "D" Coy. will march in rear of Battalion acting as rear party to collect stragglers.

4. ADMINISTRATIVE

(A) Blankets - in bundles of 10 and labelled) To be dumped
Jerkins in bundles of 10 and labelled) at Q.M. Stores by 0700.

(B) Officers Valises to be at Q.M. Stores by 0800.

(C) Coy. Mess Box and Stationery Box to be carried on Coy. Cooker and Coy. L.G.Limber.

(D) Loading Party has been detailed separately.

(E) Advance Party - 4 C.Q.M.Sr. will report to Asst. Adjt. at Orderly Room at 0745.

(F) Billets 2/Lieut. J.H.Battersby will remain behind to hand over billets.

Certificates that fire and gas precautions have been taken will be rendered to Orderly Room after arrival in billets.

5. (A) Regimental Transport. Regimental transport will follow the Battalion under the Transport Officer.

(B) Officers Chargers will be in the Square at 0900.

(C) ACKNOWLEDGE.

(signed) J.W.SWANSON Capt. & Adjt.,
15th. Battalion K.O.Y.L.I.

Issued by runner

at....1510.........

Copies to :- 1. C.O. 9. T.O.
2. Adjt. 10. I.O.
3. War Diary 11. M.O.
4-7. A. - D. Coys. 12. R.S.M.
8. Q.M. 13. 120th Infantry Brigade

№ 0

APPENDIX IV

Battalion Orders
by
Captain T.L.Webb, Commanding,
15th. Battalion King's Own Yorkshire Light Infantry

NECHIN 8/11/1918

DETAIL

Orderly Officer for tomorrow .... 2/Lieut W.J.Randles
Next for Duty .... " A.T.Ogden
Company on Duty tomorrow .... "A" Company
Next for Duty .... "B" "

696 ROUTINE

Reveille	06.30
Breakfast	07.00
Sick Parade ...	07.15
Dinners	13.00
Orderly Room ..	13.30
Tea	16.30
Lights Out	21.00

697 MEDICAL PARADES

Medical Parades will be held as follows daily :-

MORNING	"A" Coy.	07.30	"C" Coy.	07.50
	"B" "	07.40	"D" "	08.00
	Headquarters, 08.10			
AFTERNOON	"A" "	16.00	"C" "	16.30
	"B" "	16.15	"D" "	16.45
	Headquarters 16.50			

The R.S.M. will be responsible that all Officers Servants, Cooks, Orderlies etc., attend these parades.

698 TRAINING

Training Programme for 8th instant

Coy	08.30 to 09.30	09.30 to 10.30	10.45 to 11.30	11.30 to 12.30
"A"	Company Drill	Gas and Musketry.	P.T. & B.F.	Battle Formations
"B"	Deploying - Platoon in the Assault.		Gas and Musketry.	P.T. & B.F.
"C"	P.T. & B.F.	Company Drill	Battle Formations	Gas and Musketry.
"D"	Gas and Musketry.	P.T. & B.F.	Deploying - Platoon in the Assault.	

TRAINING AREAS

1. Behind "D" Coy. billets H.14.a.2.2. for ordinary parades
2. Field near Orderly Room H.14.d.5.5. for Battle Manoeuvres.

RECREATIONAL TRAINING

Inter Company Football Match H.14.a.2.2. at 14.30.

PART "C."

To The Secretary (Mob. 5d), War Office, Kew, London, S.W.1.

The above-mentioned soldier is suitable for release as a coal-miner and will be employed by .... at ....

Please arrange for his transfer to the Reserve and despatch to the address shown.

....

Date ....

Signature ....

for Controller of Coal Mines.

PART "D."

To The O.C. Discharge Centre .... Command.

The above-mentioned soldier has been ordered to report to you on .... for transfer to the Reserve for work in a coal mine.

The Deputy Adjutant General, 3rd Echelon, B.E.F., France, has been instructed to despatch to you A.F.s B.103 and 122 and the Officer i/c Records has been ordered to forward to you A.F. B.178 and 120.

The soldier will be transferred to the Reserve and despatched to the address shown in part "C" of this form.

Date ....

....

Signature, Director of Mobilization.

PART "E."

To .... (firm).

.... (address).

The soldier referred to in Part "A" of this form has been transferred to Class .... of the Reserve.

He has been despatched to you to-day.

Please complete and forward Part "F" of this form as early as possible to the address shown therein.

If at any time the soldier in question should leave your employment, you should immediately report the fact to the Secretary, War Office, Mob. 5d, Kew, London, S.W.1, stating the reasons for which he left your employment.

Date ....

.... *Rank.*

Commanding

.... *Discharge Centre.*

PART "F."

To The Secretary, War Office, Mob. 5*d*,

Kew, London, S.W. 1.

The soldier referred to in Part "A" of this form reported to me to-day.

Date ....

....

(*Signature, Colliery Firm.*)

TRAINING (continued)

N.C.Os. CLASSES - as usual.

SPECIALISTS - as usual.

699 IMMEDIATE AWARD

Divisional Order No. 2450 is repeated for information :-

"Under Authority granted by His Majesty the KING, the Field Marshal, Commanding-in-Chief, has awarded the MILITARY CROSS to the undermentioned Officer for conspicuous gallantry and devotion to duty :-

2/Lieut. F.T.Thewlis. Yorkshire Regiment
attd. King's Own Yorkshire Light Infantry.

The recipient should be informed at once and the congratulations of the Divisional and Higher Commanders conveyed to him."

700 RATION ALLOWANCE

The ration allowance for Officers and Other Ranks on leave will be 2/4d. as from the 1st November 1918.

701 N.C.Os. CLASS

Os/C. Companieswill detail four N.C.Os. instead of six as formerly to attend N.C.Os. Lewis Gun Class every afternoon. The same N.C.Os. must be sent daily to each Class.

(signed) J.W.SWANSON Capt. & Adjt.,
15th Battalion K.O.Y.L.I.

N O T I C E

The following are the amounts of dripping handed in by Units of the Brigade. 1st to 31st October 1918.

Headquarters	34 lbs	11.90 Francs.
K.O.S.Bs.	50 "	17.50 "
K.O.Y.L.I.	200 "	70.00 "
Camerons	52 "	18.20 "
120th T.M.By.	50 "	17.50 "

(*To be rendered in triplicate for each man.*)

Form A.G. 544/1 (M).

(*a*) Unit .... (*b*)* .... (*c*)* ....

RELEASE FROM THE ARMY FOR COAL-MINING (OVERSEAS).

PART "A."

No. .... Name .... Rank .... Medical Category† ....

Unit .... Corps .... Civil Occupation‡ ....

Name and address of Colliery firm with whom last employed previous to August, 1914 } ....

Period of employment with such ....

Home address ....

Mine at which last worked ....

Physical disability (if any) preventing work at his trade† ....

I am willing to be transferred to Class "W" or W(P) of the Army Reserve for the above purpose.

I certify that the above particulars are a true statement of fact.

Date ....

....
Signature of applicant.

The above particulars have been compared with the entries in Army Book 64, and I am of the opinion that the applicant was a coal-miner employed as such before August 4th, 1914.

....
Signature of O.C. Unit.

TO BE FORWARDED TO THE OFFICER COMMANDING LABOUR GROUP CONCERNED.

NOTE:—These two spaces will be filled in as follows:—
* (*b*) First three letters (in Block Capitals) of name of mine referred to in 2.
* (*c*) Name of mine in full.
e.g. (*b*) AMB.
(*c*) Ambler Thorn.
† To be verified by O.C. Unit.
‡ Insert local term for precise colliery occupation at which you were employed.

PART "B."

To Deputy Adjutant General,
3rd Echelon, G.H.Q.

I have interviewed the above-mentioned man and consider that he fulfills the conditions for release laid down, and that he should be sent home for coal-mining purposes.

Date ....

....
Interviewing Official.

A duplicate of the form will be forwarded at this stage by the interviewing official to the Controller of Coal Mines, Room 427, Holborn Viaduct Hotel, London, E.C.1, the letters P.M.E. being clearly marked in the left-hand top corner of the envelope.

PRINTED IN FRANCE BY ARMY PRINTING AND STATIONERY SERVICES. PRESS A—9/18—7984S—100,00

APPENDIX V

SECRET 9/11/18 Copy No. 3

15th Battalion K.O.Y.L.I.

MARCH ORDER NO. 3.

Ref. Maps Sheet 37 1/40.000

1. The Battalion will move to PECQ to-day.

2. ORDER OF MARCH - Starting Point - "The Church".

Companies will fall in outside present billets at 13.15. Battalion H.Q. will clear the Square at the Church at 13.30. followed by "A" "C" "D" and "B" Companies at intervals of 100 yards.

3. DRESS - full marching order with packs, S.B.Rs. slung, Steel helmets to be worn. Water Bottles to be filled before marching off.

Second in Command will ride in rear of Battalion.

One Subaltern and two N.C.Os. to be detailed by O/C "A" Company will act as rear party.

4. ADMINISTRATIVE

(A) BLANKETS in bundles of 10 and labelled
JERKINS in bundles of 10 and labelled

to be dumped at Shoemakers Shop immediately.

(B) Officers Valises - to be dumped at shoemakers shop immediately.

(C) Company Mess Box and Stationery Box to be carried as usual.

(D) Loading Party has been detailed separately.

5. Regimental Transport will follow the Battalion under the Transport Officer.

Lewis Gun Limbers will follow Companies.

Officers Chargers to report to Company Commanders ~~xxxxxxx~~ immediately.

(signed) J.W.SWANSON Capt. and Adjt.
15th Battalion K.O.Y.L.I.

Copies to :-

1. C.O.
2. Adjt.
3. War Diary
4-7. "A" to "D" Coys.
8. Q.M.
9. T.O.
10. I.O.
11. M.O.
12. R.S.M.
13. 120th Inf. Bde.

Issued by Runner at ....

(To be rendered in triplicate for each man.)

Form A.G. 544/1 (M).

(a) Unit .... (b)* .... (c)* ....

RELEASE FROM THE ARMY FOR COAL-MINING (OVERSEAS).

PART "A."

No. .... Name .... Rank .... Medical Category† ....

Unit .... Corps .... Civil Occupation‡ ....

Name and address of Colliery firm with whom last employed previous to August, 1914 ....

Period of employment with such ....

Home address ....

Mine at which last worked ....

Physical disability (if any) preventing work at his trade† ....

I am willing to be transferred to Class "W" or W(P) of the Army Reserve for the above purpose.

I certify that the above particulars are a true statement of fact.

Date ....

Signature of applicant.

The above particulars have been compared with the entries in Army Book 64, and I am of the opinion that the applicant was a coal-miner employed as such before August 4th, 1914.

....

Signature of O.C. Unit.

TO BE FORWARDED TO THE OFFICER COMMANDING LABOUR GROUP CONCERNED.

NOTE:—These two spaces will be filled in as follows:—

* (b) First three letters (in Block Capitals) of name of mine referred to in 2.
* (c) Name of mine in full.
e.g. (b) AMB.
(c) Ambler Thorn.

† To be verified by O.C. Unit.
‡ Insert local term for precise colliery occupation at which you were employed.

PART "B."

To Deputy Adjutant General,
3rd Echelon, G.H.Q.

I have interviewed the above-mentioned man and consider that he fulfills the conditions for release laid down, and that he should be sent home for coal-mining purposes.

Date ....

Interviewing Official.

A duplicate of the form will be forwarded at this stage by the interviewing official to the Controller of Coal Mines, Room 427, Holborn Viaduct Hotel, London, E.C.1, the letters P.M.E. being clearly marked in the left-hand top corner of the envelope.

PRINTED IN FRANCE BY ARMY PRINTING AND STATIONERY SERVICES. PRESS A—9/18—7984S—100,000.

APPENDIX VI

Battalion Orders
by
Lieut-Colonel T.N.T.Isaac,
Commanding 15th Battalion King's Own Yorkshire Light Infantry.

HESDIGNEUL. 11/11/18.

DETAIL.

Orderly Officer tomorrow .... 2/Lieut J.Fox,
Next for Duty .... " J.H.Battersby
Company on Duty tomorrow .... "D" Company
Next for Duty .... "A" "

712 ROUTINE

Reveille 06.30
Breakfast 07.00
Sick Parade 07.15
Orderly Room 12.00
Dinners 12.30
Tea 16.30
Retreat 16.50
Lights Out 21.00

713 HOSTILITIES.

AN ARMISTICE HAVING BEEN SIGNED, HOSTILITIES BETWEEN THE ALLIED POWERS AND GERMANY CEASED TO-DAY AT 11.00 HOURS.

714 MEDICAL PARADES

Medical Parades will be held as follows daily :-

	"A" Coy.	07.20	"C" Coy.	07.50
MORNING	"B" "	07.40	"D" "	08.00
		Headquarters 08.10		
	"A" "	16.00	"C" "	16.30
AFTERNOON	"B" "	16.15	"D" "	16.45
		Headquarters 16.50		

All Officers will arrange direct with the M.O. to "gargle" twice daily.

The C.S.M. will be responsible that all Officers Servants, Cooks, Orderlies, etc attend these parades.

715 TRAINING.

CANCELLED.

716 GERMAN RIFLE CARTRIDGES.

A number of German Rifle Cartridges with wooden bullets have beenleft behind in old German Machine Gun Emplacements.
Troops must be warned against using these cartridges for either rifle or machine gun exercises, as, although they appear very much the same as our own dummy cartridges, they contain a small charge and are quite capable, if fired at short range, of inflicting serious injuries.
(IV Corps Routine Orders No. 1784 dated 10/11/18)

(Signed) J.H.STANTON Capt. & Adjt.,
15th Battalion K.O.Y.L.I.

PART "C."

To The Secretary (Mob. 5d), War Office, Kew, London, S.W.1.

The above-mentioned soldier is suitable for release as a coal-miner and will be employed by .... at ....

Please arrange for his transfer to the Reserve and despatch to the address shown.

Date.. *Signature* ....
for Controller of Coal Mines.

PART "D."

To The O.C. Discharge Centre .... Command.

The above-mentioned soldier has been ordered to report to you on .... for transfer to the Reserve for work in a coal mine.

The Deputy Adjutant General, 3rd Echelon, B.E.F., France, has been instructed to despatch to you A.F.s B.103 and 122 and the Officer i/c Records has been ordered to forward to you A.F. B.178 and 120.

The soldier will be transferred to the Reserve and despatched to the address shown in part "C" of this form.

Date..
Signature, Director of Mobilization.

PART "E."

To ....(firm).

....(address).

The soldier referred to in Part "A" of this form has been transferred to Class .... of the Reserve.

He has been despatched to you to-day.

Please complete and forward Part "F" of this form as early as possible to the address shown therein.

If at any time the soldier in question should leave your employment, you should immediately report the fact to the Secretary, War Office, Mob. 5d, Kew, London, S.W.1, stating the reasons for which he left your employment.

Date.. ....*Rank.*

Commanding

....*Discharge Centre.*

PART "F."

To The Secretary, War Office, Mob. *5d*,
Kew, London, S.W. 1.

The soldier referred to in Part "A" of this form reported to me to day.

Date ....
(Signature, Colliery Firm.)

12-11-18 APPENDIX VII

SECRET 15th Battalion K.O.Y.L.I. Copy No.....3....

MARCH ORDER No. 4.

Ref.Maps Sheet 37 1/40.000

1. The Battalion will move to BUCQUOI tomorrow.

2. Order of March. Starting Point - Cemetery Gates.

Battalion will parade facing South on road at 09.20 as follows :- Battn. H.Q. with head of column at Cemetery Gates, "B" Company, "A" Coy. "D" Coy. "C" Coy. at ten yards interval.

Battalion H.Q. will pass the starting point at 09.29. Intervals laid down in F.S.R. will be maintained.

3. Dress. Full Marching Order with Packs, S.B.Rs. Slung. Water Bottles to be filled before marching off. Steel helmets will not be carried.

Captain P.Fisher will act as Second in Command and will ride in rear of the Battalion. One Subaltern and two N.C.Os. to be detailed by O/C "A" Company will act as rear party.

4. ADMINISTRATIVE

(A) Blankets rolled in bundles of 10 and labelled
Jerkins in bundles of 10 and labelled
Steel helmets in tens and labelled

Will be dumped at present Coy. H.Q. under cover under one N.C.O, and two men per Coy.

(B) Loading Party O/C "B" Company will detail one N.C.O. and four men to report to Q.M. at 07.45. Dress. Full marching Order less steel helmet.

(C) Officers Valises To be at Q.M. Stores at 07.45.

(D) Company Mess Box and Stationery Box to be carried as usual.

(E) Advance Party four C.Q.M.Ss. will report to R.S.M. at Orderly Room at 08.15.

5. TRANSPORT

(A) Lewis Gun Limbers will follow Companies.
(B) Officers Chargers will report to Companies at 08.30.

REGIMENTAL TRANSPORT

"A" Echelon will follow Battalion. "B" and "C" Echelons as detailed separately.

6. Acknowledge.

(signed) J.W.SWANSON Capt. & Adjt
15th Battalion K.O.Y.L.I.

Copies to :-

1. C.O.
2. Adjt.
3. War Diary
4-7. "A" to "D" Coys.
8. Q.M.
9. T.O.
10. Signalling Officer
11. M.O.
12. R.S.M.
13. 120th Inf. Bde.

Issued by Runner at ..2300..

PART "C."

To The Secretary (Mob. 5d), War Office, Kew, London, S.W.1.

The above-mentioned soldier is suitable for release as a coal-miner and will be employed by .... at ....

Please arrange for his transfer to the Reserve and despatch to the address shown.

Date.................................... *Signature* ....

for Controller of Coal Mines.

PART "D."

To The O.C. Discharge Centre.............................. Command.

The above-mentioned soldier has been ordered to report to you on.............................. for transfer to the Reserve for work in a coal mine.

The Deputy Adjutant General, 3rd Echelon, B.E.F., France, has been instructed to despatch to you A.F.s B.103 and 122 and the Officer i/c Records has been ordered to forward to you A.F. B.178 and 120.

The soldier will be transferred to the Reserve and despatched to the address shown in part "C" of this form.

Date....................................

Signature, Director of Mobilization.

PART "E."

To .... (firm).

.... (address).

The soldier referred to in Part "A" of this form has been transferred to Class.............. of the Reserve.

He has been despatched to you to-day.

Please complete and forward Part "F" of this form as early as possible to the address shown therein.

If at any time the soldier in question should leave your employment, you should immediately report the fact to the Secretary, War Office, Mob. 5d, Kew, London, S.W.1, stating the reasons for which he left your employment.

Date.................................... .... *Rank.*

Commanding

.... *Discharge Centre.*

PART "F."

To The Secretary, War Office, Mob. 5*d*,
Kew, London, S.W. 1.

The soldier referred to in Part "A" of this form reported to me to-day.

Date.................................... ....

(*Signature, Colliery Firm.*)

APPENDIX VIII

Battalion Orders,
by
Lieut-Colonel T.W.T.Isaac,
Commanding 15th Battalion King's Own Yorkshire Light Infantry

BUCQUOI 14/11/18.

DETAIL

Orderly Officer tomorrow	2/Lieut. W.R.Ashton
Next for Duty..........................	" N.C.Moore
Company on Duty tomorrow............	"C" Company,
Next for Duty..........................	"D" "

730 ROUTINE

Reveille.............	06.30
Breakfast	07.00
Sick Parade.........	07.15
Orderly Room	12.00
Dinners	12.39
Teas................	16.30
RRETREAT............	16.50
Lights Out..........	21.00

731 MEDICAL PARADES

"A" Coy.	07.30	"C" Coy.	07.50
"B" "	07.40	"D" "	08.00
Headquarters 08.10			
"A" "	16.00	"C" "	16.30
"B" "	16.15	"D" "	16.45
Headquarters 16.50			

All Officers will arrange direct with the M.O. to "gargle" twice daily.

The R.S.M. will be responsible that all Officers Servants, Cooks, Orderlies etc., attend these parades.

732 DRAFT

A Draft of 69 other ranks joined the Battalion 13/11/18 and posted to Companies as follows :-

"A" Company	22 Other Ranks
"B" "	4 N.C.Os. 25 Other Ranks
"C" "	13 Other Ranks
"D" "	5 Other Ranks

The draft will report sick on Sick Parade tomorrow morning.

Date .... *Signature* ....

for Controller of Coal Mines.

PART "D."

To The O.C. Discharge Centre .... Command.

The above-mentioned soldier has been ordered to report to you on .... for transfer to the Reserve for work in a coal mine.

The Deputy Adjutant General, 3rd Echelon, B.E.F., France, has been instructed to despatch to you A.F.s B.103 and 122 and the Officer i/c Records has been ordered to forward to you A.F. B.178 and 120.

The soldier will be transferred to the Reserve and despatched to the address shown in part "C" of this form.

Date ....

Signature, Director of Mobilization.

PART "E."

To .... (firm).

.... (address).

The soldier referred to in Part "A" of this form has been transferred to Class .... of the Reserve.

He has been despatched to you to-day.

Please complete and forward Part "F" of this form as early as possible to the address shown therein.

If at any time the soldier in question should leave your employment, you should immediately report the fact to the Secretary, War Office, Mob. 5d, Kew, London, S.W.1, stating the reasons for which he left your employment.

Date .... *Rank.*

Commanding

.... *Discharge Centre.*

PART "F."

To The Secretary, War Office, Mob. *5d*,
Kew, London, S.W. 1.

The soldier referred to in Part "A" of this form reported to me to-day.

Date ....

(Signature, Colliery Firm.)

735 TRAINING

08.30 - 09.30	Company Commander's Inspection.
09.30 - 10.30	Battalion Parade at G.24.b.1.8.
10.30	Brigade Ceremonial parade at G.30.c.Central.

NOTE - BRIGADE CEREMONIAL PARADE

The Battalion will be formed up in close column of Companies at 10.30 at G.30.c.

DRESS - as to-day.

Officers and men of the Trench Mortar Battery will attend the Battalion Parade as above, and will proceed with the Battalion to Brigade Ceremonial Parade.

Officers Servants and Company Clerks will attend these parades tomorrow.

Companies will render to the Adjutant by 09.00 WITHOUT FAIL a parade State showing numbers on parade by ranks.

The Instructions for the procedure at Ceremonial Parades issued to Companies tonight will be strictly adhered to.

BATTALION SPORTS

Battalion Sports will be held tomorrow at G.24.~~b.1.8~~ a.3.6.

Separate Programmes will be issued later.

The Divisional Band will be in attendance.

(signed) J.W.SWANSON Capt. & Adjt.,
15th Battalion K.O.Y.L.I.

(To be rendered in triplicate for each man.)

Form A.G. 544/1 (M).

(a) Unit .... *(b)** .... *(c)** ....

RELEASE FROM THE ARMY FOR COAL-MINING (OVERSEAS).

PART "A."

No. .... Name .... Rank .... Medical Category† ....

Unit .... Corps .... Civil Occupation‡ ....

Name and address of Colliery firm with whom last employed previous to August, 1914 ....

Period of employment with such ....

Home address ....

Mine at which last worked ....

Physical disability (if any) preventing work at his trade† ....

I am willing to be transferred to Class "W" or W(P) of the Army Reserve for the above purpose.

I certify that the above particulars are a true statement of fact.

Date ....

Signature of applicant.

The above particulars have been compared with the entries in Army Book 64, and I am of the opinion that the applicant was a coal-miner employed as such before August 4th, 1914.

....

Signature of O.C. Unit.

TO BE FORWARDED TO THE OFFICER COMMANDING LABOUR GROUP CONCERNED.

NOTE :—These two spaces will be filled in as follows :—

* *(b)* First three letters (in Block Capitals) of name of mine referred to in 2.

* *(c)* Name of mine in full.

e.g. *(b)* AMB.

(c) Ambler Thorn.

† To be verified by O.C. Unit.

‡ Insert local term for precise colliery occupation at which you were employed.

PART "B."

To Deputy Adjutant General,

3rd Echelon, G.H.Q.

I have interviewed the above-mentioned man and consider that he fulfills the conditions for release laid down, and that he should be sent home for coal-mining purposes.

Date ....

Interviewing Official.

A duplicate of the form will be forwarded at this stage by the interviewing official to the Controller of Coal Mines, Room 427, Holborn Viaduct Hotel, London, E.C.1, the letters P.M.E. being clearly marked in the left-hand top corner of the envelope.

PRINTED IN FRANCE BY ARMY PRINTING AND STATIONERY SERVICES. PRESS A—2/18—7981S—100,000.

APPENDIX IX

Battalion Orders
by
Lieut-Colonel T.W.T.Isaac,
Commanding 15th Battalion King's Own Yorkshire Light Infantry

BUCQUOI 14/11/18

DETAIL

Orderly Officer tomorrow	2/Lieut W.R.Ashton
Next for Duty	" N.C.Moors
Company on Duty tomorrow	"C" Company
Next for Duty	"D" "

730 ROUTINE

Reveille	06.30
Breakfast............	07.00
Sick Parade	07.15
Orderly Room	12.00
Dinners	12.30
Teas	16.30
RETREAT..............	16.30
Lights Out	21.00

731 MEDICAL PARADES

"A" Coy.	07.30	"C" Coy.	07.50
"B" "	07.40	"D" "	08.00
	Headquarters 08.10		
"A" "	16.00	"C" "	16.30
"B" "	16.15	"D" "	16.45
	Headquarters 16.50		

All Officers will arrange direct with the M.O. to "gargle" twice daily.

The R.S.M. will be responsible that all Officers Servants Cooks, Orderlies etc., attend these parades.

732 DRAFT

A draft of 69 other ranks joined the Battalion 13/11/18 and were posted to Companies as follows :-

"A" Company		22 Other Ranks
"B" "	4 N.C.Os.	25 " "
"C" "		13 " "
"D" "		5 " "

The draft will report sick on Sick Parade tomorrow morni

Unit .... Corps .... Civil Occupation‡ ....

Name and address of Colliery firm with whom last employed previous to August, 1914 ....

Period of employment with such ....

Home address ....

Mine at which last worked ....

Physical disability (if any) preventing work at his trade† ....

I am willing to be transferred to Class "W" or W(P) of the Army Reserve for the above purpose.

I certify that the above particulars are a true statement of fact.

Date ....

Signature of applicant.

The above particulars have been compared with the entries in Army Book 64, and I am of the opinion that the applicant was a coal-miner employed as such before August 4th, 1914.

Signature of O.C. Unit.

TO BE FORWARDED TO THE OFFICER COMMANDING LABOUR GROUP CONCERNED

NOTE:—These two spaces will be filled in as follows:—

* (*b*) First three letters (in Block Capitals) of name of mine referred to in 2.
* (*c*) Name of mine in full.
e.g. (*b*) AMB.
(*c*) Ambler Thorn.
† To be verified by O.C. Unit.
‡ Insert local term for precise colliery occupation at which you were employed.

PART "B."

To Deputy Adjutant General,
3rd Echelon, G.H.Q.

I have interviewed the above-mentioned man and consider that he fulfills the conditions for release laid down, and that he should be sent home for coal-mining purposes.

Date ....

Interviewing Official.

A duplicate of the form will be forwarded at this stage by the interviewing official to the Controller of Coal Mines, Room 127, Holborn Viaduct Hotel, London, E.C.1, the letters P.M.E. being clearly marked in the left-hand top corner of the envelope.

PRINTED IN FRANCE BY ARMY PRINTING AND STATIONERY SERVICES PRESS A—9/18—7984S—100,000.

3 TRAINING

08.30 - 09.30	Company Commander's Inspection
09.30 - 10.30	Battn. Parade at G.24.b.1.8.
10.30	Brigade Ceremonial Parade at G.30.c.Central

NOTE. BRIGADE CEREMONIAL PARADE

The Battalion will be formed up in close column of Companies at 10.30 at G.30.c.

Dress - as to-day.

Officers and men of the Trench Mortar Battery will attend the Battalion Parade as above, and will proceed with the Battalion to Brigade Ceremonial Parade.

Officers Servants and Company Clerks will attend these parades tomorrow.

Companies will render to the Adjutant by 09.00 WITHOUT FAIL a Parade State showing numbers on parade by ranks.

The instructions for the procedure at Ceremonial Parades issued to Companies tonight will be strictly adhered to.

BATTALION SPORTS

Battalion Sports will be held tomorrow at G.24.~~b.1.8~~ a.8.6.. Separate Programmes will be issued later.

The Divisional Band will be in attendance.

(signed) J.W.SWANSON Capt. & Adjt.,
15th Battalion K.O.Y.L.I.

PART "C."

To The Secretary (Mob. 5d), War Office, Kew, London, S.W.1.

The above-mentioned soldier is suitable for release as a coal-miner and will be employed by .... at ....

Please arrange for his transfer to the Reserve and despatch to the address shown.

....

Date.. *Signature* ....
for Controller of Coal Mines.

PART "D."

To The O.C. Discharge Centre .... Command.

The above-mentioned soldier has been ordered to report to you on .... for transfer to the Reserve for work in a coal mine.

The Deputy Adjutant General, 3rd Echelon, B.E.F., France, has been instructed to despatch to you A.F.s B.103 and 122 and the Officer i/c Records has been ordered to forward to you A.F. B.178 and 120.

The soldier will be transferred to the Reserve and despatched to the address shown in part "C" of this form.

Date.. ....
Signature, Director of Mobilization.

PART "E."

To .... (firm).

.... (address).

The soldier referred to in Part "A" of this form has been transferred to Class .... of the Reserve.

He has been despatched to you to-day.

Please complete and forward Part "F" of this form as early as possible to the address shown therein.

If at any time the soldier in question should leave your employment, you should immediately report the fact to the Secretary, War Office, Mob. 5d, Kew, London, S.W.1, stating the reasons for which he left your employment.

Date.. .... *Rank.*
Commanding
.... *Discharge Centre.*

PART "F."

To The Secretary, War Office, Mob. 5*d*,
Kew, London, S.W. 1.

The soldier referred to in Part "A" of this form reported to me to-day.

Date.. ....
(Signature, Colliery Firm.)

APPENDIX X

Battalion Orders
by
Lieut-Colonel T.W.T.Isaac,
Commanding 15th Battalion King's Own Yorkshire Light Infantry

BUCQUOY 15/11/18

Orderly Officer tomorrow ....2/Lieut. N.C.Moore
Next for Duty ....2/Lieut. J.A.Williams
Company on Duty tomorrow ...."D" Company
Next for Duty ...."A" Company

734 ROUTINE

Reveille 06.30
Breakfast 07.00
Sick Parade...... 07.15
Orderly Room 12.00
Dinners.......... 12.30
Teas 16.30
RETREAT.......... 16.30
Lights Out 21.00

735 MEDICAL PARADES

Battalion Medical Parades will be held tomorrow as follows :-

"A" Company 07.30 "C" Company 07.50
"B" " 07.40 "D" " 08.00
Headquarters 08.10

All Officers will arrange direct withbthe M.O. to "gargle" daily.

The R.S.M. will be responsible that all Officers Servants Cooks, Orderlies etc., attend these parades.

736 TRAINING

08.30 to 09.00 Company Commander's Inspection
09.20 Battalion Parade. G.24.b.1.8.

1. BATTALION PARADE

(a) DRESS = Marching Order with Packs. Steel Helmets and S.B.Rs. will not be carried.

(b) DETAIL = Personnel of the Trench Mortar Battery will attend this parade, and will be attached to Companies as to-day.

Four markers per Coy. report on ground to R.S.M. at 09.10.

Battalion will be formed up in mass.

There will be a BRIGADE ROUTE MARCH tomorrow. The Battalion will join the column at cross roads at H.13.d.7.6. at 10.03. The intervals laid down in F.S.R. will be maintained between Coys.

The Band will attend this parade.

2. (a) "A" Echelon will follow the Battalion on line of march, and will be lined up on road near G.24.b.1.8. at 09.30.

(b) Lewis Gun Limbers will follow Companies.

(*To be rendered in triplicate for each man.*)

Form A.G. 544/1 (M).

(*a*) Unit .... (*b*)* .... (*c*)* ....

RELEASE FROM THE ARMY FOR COAL-MINING (OVERSEAS).

PART "A."

No. .... Name .... Rank .... Medical Category† ....

Unit .... Corps .... Civil Occupation‡ ....

Name and address of Colliery firm with whom last employed previous to August, 1914 ....

Period of employment with such ....

Home address ....

Mine at which last worked ....

Physical disability (if any) preventing work at his trade† ....

I am willing to be transferred to Class "W" or W(P) of the Army Reserve for the above purpose.

I certify that the above particulars are a true statement of fact.

Date ....

Signature of applicant.

The above particulars have been compared with the entries in Army Book 64, and I am of the opinion that the applicant was a coal-miner employed as such before August 4th, 1914.

....

Signature of O.C. Unit.

TO BE FORWARDED TO THE OFFICER COMMANDING LABOUR GROUP CONCERNED.

NOTE:—These two spaces will be filled in as follows:—

* (*b*) First three letters (in Block Capitals) of name of mine referred to in 2.
* (*c*) Name of mine in full.
e.g. (*b*) AMB.
(*c*) Ambler Thorn.

† To be verified by O.C. Unit.
‡ Insert local term for precise colliery occupation at which you were employed.

PART "B."

To Deputy Adjutant General,
3rd Echelon, G.H.Q.

I have interviewed the above-mentioned man and consider that he fulfills the conditions for release laid down, and that he should be sent home for coal-mining purposes.

Date ....

Interviewing Official.

A duplicate of the form will be forwarded at this stage by the interviewing official to the Controller of Coal Mines, Room 427, Holborn Viaduct Hotel, London, E.C.1, the letters P.M.E. being clearly marked in the left-hand top corner of the envelope.

PRINTED IN FRANCE BY ARMY PRINTING AND STATIONERY SERVICES PRESS A—9/18—7984S—100,000.

737 DIVISIONAL PATCHES

O/C. Coys. will arrange for small batches of N.C.Os. and men who are not wearing the Divisional Patch, to attend at Tailors' Shop after parades.

(signed) J.W.SWANSON Capt. & Adjt.,
15th Battalion K.O.Y.L.I.

Padre

APPENDIX X-1

Battalion Orders,
by
Lieut-Colonel T.W.T.Isaac,
Commanding 15th Battalion King's Own Yorkshire Light Infantry

---

BUCQUOI 16/11/18

DETAIL

Orderly Officer tomorrow .... 2/Lieut J.A.Williams
Next for Duty .... " J.C.Waterton
Company on Duty tomorrow .... "A" Company
Next for Duty .... "B" "

738 ROUTINE

Reveille	07.00
Breakfast	07.45
Sick Parade	08.00
Dinners............	12.30
Tea................	16.00
RETREAT............	16.30
Lights Out.........	21.00

739 MEDICAL PARADES

Medical Parades will be held tomorrow as follows :-

"A" Company	08.15	"C" Company	0835
"B" "	08.25	"D" "	08.50

Headquarters 08.55.

All Officers will arrange direct with the M.O. to "gargle" daily.

The R.S.M. will be responsible that all Officers Servants, Cooks, Orderlies etc attend these parades.

740 APPOINTMENT

The undermentioned appointment is made :-

T/Capt. T.L.Webb to be Acting Major with effect from 24/10/18 while acting as Second-in-Command.
(Authority 40th Div. 848.A. dated 13/11/18)

741 DIVINE SERVICE

The Battalion will parade for Divine Service tomorrow as follows :-

C.of Es. Parade in field at G.22.b.7.3. (near H.Q.Mess) at 09.30. Right Markers report on ground to R.S.M.at 09.20.

Dress - Drill Order with rifles. The band will attend.

Parade will march to "Gamecocks" Hall at LANNOY where a Service will be held at 10.00.

Presbyterians and Non-Conformists parade as above at 11.10. The Orderly Officer will march this party to K.O.S.B. Parade Ground.

742 DUTIES.

Until further Orders the Orderly Officer will mount the Brigade Guard daily at 08.00.

743 OFFICERS' POSTINGS

The following extracts are taken from "Supplement to London Gazette" dated 13th Novr. 1918.

Infantry,
Service Battalions
K.O.Y.L.I

" Major H.J.R.Bock (High.L.I. T.F.) is apptd to a Bn. (May 28, sen. Nov. 3, 1914). The follg. Capts. are apptd to a Bn. :- A.Lindemere (L'pool R., Spec. Res) (late Lt. Res. of Off.) (May 28. sen Nov 10.1914) Capt. L.M. Sandison (K.O. Sco.Bord., Spec.Res) is apptd to a Bn. (sen.Nov.9.1914) and to be Adjt. (May 28); Temp.Capt. G.N.Watney, from LabCorps to be Temp.Capt. Sen.May 21.1915); Temp Capt T.L.Webb from York. R. (attd) to be temp. Capt (June 29, sen Nov. 14.1914); Temp. Lt. W.R.Pearson from Lab.Corps to be temp. Lt. sen. July 1st 1917); Temp. Lt. R.S.Walters from Lab.Corps to be temp. Lt. (June 10, sen. Dec. 27, 1916) Sec.Lts G.Blewitt (York.R. T.F) is apptd. to a Bn. June 29, sen. May 1) Temp. Sec. Lts. from Lab.Corps to be temp. Sec.Lts. sen. specified against their names:- C.F.Beeching (May 15.1917) C.P.Prest (Aug.19.1917) J.W.Swanson (Sept 1.1917) F.L.Blagden (April 2). Temp.Sec. Lts. from Lab.Corps to be temp.Sec.Lts. (June 10 sen. specified against their names :- H.E.Basden (Sept.13.1917) G.L.R. Brown (Sept. 16.1917); B.O.Denham (Oct. 19.1917) G.W.W.Dron (Oct 20.1917)

744 DISCIPLINE

It has been reported that Officers proceeding on leave from this Brigade have not reported to the Divisional Reception Camp. If any further reports are received it will be necessary to consider the suspension of leave for Officers.

745 OFFICERS

All Officers will forward to Orderly Room by 14.00 tomorrow their "Officers Record of Service Book" (A.B.439).

746 APPOINTMENTS

The following extract from the Supplement to London Gazette dated November 14th 1918 is published for information :-

Infantry
Service Battalions
K.O.Y.L.I

Capt.L.M.Sandison (K.O.Sco.Bord., Spec.Res) to be Temp.Major (June 11). Temp.Sec.Lts. to be Temp. Capts. J.W.Swanson (June 11); A.Morrow from R.Dub.Fus. (attd) (Aug 2.).

(signed) J.W.SWANSON Capt. & Adjt.,
15th Battalion K.O.Y.L.I.

N O T I C E

The following Voluntary Services will be held tomrrow :-

C. of Es.	Holy Communion in the Y.M.C.A.	08.15
	Evening Service in the Y.M.C.A.	18.30
	Holy Communion	19.30

Copies to 120th Inf Bde
TMB

APPENDIX XII

Battalion Orders
by
Lieut-Colonel T.W.T.Isaac,
Commanding 15th Battalion King's Own Yorkshire Light Infantry

BUCQUOI 17/11/18

DETAIL
Orderly Officer tomorrow .... 2/Lieut. J.C.Waterton
Next for Duty .... 2/Lieut. J.H.Battersby
Company on Duty tomorrow .... "B" Company
Next for Duty .... "C" Company

747 ROUTINE

Reveille 06.30
Breakfast........ 07.00
Sick Parade 07.15
Orderly Room 12.00
Dinners.......... 12.30
Teas............. 16.30
RETREAT 16.30
Lights Out....... 21.00

748 MEDICAL PARADES

Medical parades will be held tomorrow as follows :-

"A" Company	07.30	"C" Company	07.50
"B" "	07.40	"D" "	08.00
	Headquarters 08.10		

All Officers will arrange direct with the M.O. to "gargle" daily. The R.S.M. will be responsible that all Officers Servants, Cooks, Orderlies etc., attend these parades.

749 TRAINING

08.15	Company Commanders Parade
08.45	Battalion Parade at G.24.b.1.8.
10.00	Brigade Ceremonial parade at H.14.d. (nr. former Orderly Room at NECHIN)

Battalion will parade at G.24.b.1.8. in close column of Companies. Dress - drill order with rifles. All men will wear jerkins, and Officers will wear British Warms or Trench Coats. One marker per Company to report to R.S.M. on ground at G.24.b.1.8. at 08.40.

750 RETURN - GERMAN SPEAKING OFFICERS & MEN.

Os/C. Coys. will forward to Orderly Room by 18.00 tomorrow nominal roll of Officers and other ranks who can speak German fluently. They will probably be required as interpreters during the occupation of "RHINELAND".

751 FIRE PRECAUTIONS

Attention is drawn to G.R.O. 2717. The instructions laid down are to be carefully observed so far as they apply to present circumstances.

752 ACCIDENTAL & SELF INFLICTED WOUNDS - DANGER OF TAMPERING WITH BOMBS, DETONATORS, ETC.

G.R.O. 1749 dated 16/11/18 is published for information :-

"Attention is drawn to G.R.O. 1668. Cases have occurred of individuals injuring themselves through tampering with Bombs and Detonators which have been found lying about.

In some cases the injured man has produced as a plea that he did not know what the article was. All ranks are

PART "C."

To The Secretary (Mob. 5d), War Office, Kew, London, S.W.1.

The above-mentioned soldier is suitable for release as a coal-miner and will be employed by .... at ....

Please arrange for his transfer to the Reserve and despatch to the address shown.

....

Date........................ *Signature*..

for Controller of Coal Mines.

PART "D."

To The O.C. Discharge Centre........................Command.

The above-mentioned soldier has been ordered to report to you on........................ for transfer to the Reserve for work in a coal mine.

The Deputy Adjutant General, 3rd Echelon, B.E.F., France, has been instructed to despatch to you A.F.s B.103 and 122 and the Officer i/c Records has been ordered to forward to you A.F. B.178 and 120.

The soldier will be transferred to the Reserve and despatched to the address shown in part "C" of this form.

Date........................

....

Signature, Director of Mobilization.

PART "E."

To..(firm).

....(address).

The soldier referred to in Part "A" of this form has been transferred to Class........................ of the Reserve.

He has been despatched to you to-day.

Please complete and forward Part "F" of this form as early as possible to the address shown therein.

If at any time the soldier in question should leave your employment, you should immediately report the fact to the Secretary, War Office, Mob. 5d, Kew, London, S.W.1, stating the reasons for which he left your employment.

Date........................ ....*Rank.*

Commanding

....*Discharge Centre.*

PART "F."

To The Secretary, War Office, Mob. 5*d*,
Kew, London, S.W. 1.

The soldier referred to in Part "A" of this form reported to me to-day.

Date........................ ....

(*Signature, Colliery Firm.*)

752 (continued)

therefore warned not to tamper with articles found lying about in areas recently occupied by the enemy but to report their existence to proper authority who will arrange for their removal by experts.......

753 RETURN - RAILWAY PERSONNEL

Os/c. Coys. will forward to Orderly Room by 18.00 ~~xxxxxxxx~~ 19th instant the names of all Officers and other ranks who have had ~~a railway~~ technical experience in any of the following trades on railways in Great Britain.
ALL NAMES MUST BE FORWARDED WITHOUT FAIL.

Blacksmiths, Ordinary
" Strikers

Blockmen
Boilermakers
Boilersmiths
Brickarchmen
Carpenters & Joiners
Clerks, General Railway
" Stenographers with Railway experience
" Timekeepers
Controllers.
Draughtsmen, Mechanical Loco.
Engine Drivers Loco.
Firemen, Loco.
Fitters, Electric
" Loco.
" Mechanists
" Westinghouse Brake.
Guards & Brakesmen.
Yardmasters
Wagon erectors & Repairers.

Machinemen, Drillers
" Grinders
" Slotters & Planers

Turners, Brass
" Iron
" General
Millwrights

Pioneers, Boilerwashers

Pioneers, Cleaners
" Numbertakers
" Porters
" Pumpers
" Steam raisers
Shunters
Stationmasters
Storekeepers
Tubers

(signed) J.W.SWANSON Capt. & Adjt.,
15th Battalion K.O.Y.L.I.

PART "C."

To The Secretary (Mob. 5d), War Office, Kew, London, S.W.1.

The above-mentioned soldier is suitable for release as a coal-miner and will be employed by .... at ....

Please arrange for his transfer to the Reserve and despatch to the address shown.

....

Date.................................. *Signature*..
for Controller of Coal Mines.

PART "D."

To The O.C. Discharge Centre.................................. Command.

The above-mentioned soldier has been ordered to report to you on.................................. for transfer to the Reserve for work in a coal mine.

The Deputy Adjutant General, 3rd Echelon, B.E.F., France, has been instructed to despatch to you A.F.s B.103 and 122 and the Officer i/c Records has been ordered to forward to you A.F. B.178 and 120.

The soldier will be transferred to the Reserve and despatched to the address shown in part "C" of this form.

Date.................................. ....
Signature, Director of Mobilization.

PART "E."

To.. (firm).

.... (address).

The soldier referred to in Part "A" of this form has been transferred to Class.................. of the Reserve.

He has been despatched to you to-day.

Please complete and forward Part "F" of this form as early as possible to the address shown therein.

If at any time the soldier in question should leave your employment, you should immediately report the fact to the Secretary, War Office, Mob. 5d, Kew, London, S.W.1, stating the reasons for which he left your employment.

Date.................................. .... *Rank.*
Commanding

.... *Discharge Centre.*

PART "F."

To The Secretary, War Office, Mob. 5*d*,
Kew, London, S.W. 1.

The soldier referred to in Part "A" of this form reported to me to-day.

Date.................................. ....
(Signature, Colliery Firm.)

6.

APPENDIX XIII

Battalion Orders
by
Lieut-Colonel T.W.T.ICAAM,
Commanding 15th Battalion King's Own Yorkshire Light Infantry

BUCQUOI

1[illegible]/11/18

DETAIL

Orderly Officer tomorrow .... 2/Lieut. W.R.Ashton
Next for Duty .... " J.Fox
Company on Duty tomorrow .... "C" Company
Next for Duty .... "D" "

4 ROUTINE

Reveille 06.30
Breakfast 07.00
Sick Parade 07.15
Orderly Room ...... Will be notified later.
Dinners 12.30
Teas 16.30
RETREAT 16.30
Lights Out 21.00

5 MEDICAL PARADES

There will be NO Medical Parades tomorrow.

56 PARADES

08.15 Company Commanders Parade.
08.45 Battalion Parade at G.24.b.1.8.
10.00 Brigade Ceremonial Parade at H.14.d.

Battn. will parade at G.24.b.1.8. in close column of Coys. DRESS - Drill Order with rifles. All men will wear jerkins and Officers will wear British Warms or Trench Coats. Officers will NOT carry sticks.

One marker per Company to report to R.S.M. on ground at G.24.b.1.8. at 08.40. Companies to be sized before marching on Battalion Parade Ground.

The Corps Commander will inspect the Brigade at 11.00 on parade ground at H.14.d.

All transport (as detailed separately) will parade behind "D" Company.

57 BATHS

The Baths at NECHIN are allotted to Companies tomorrow as follows :-

"A" Coy. 14.00 - 15.00 "B" Coy. 15.00 - 16.00

Parties of fifty will be sent each half hour.
Clean clothes will be available at the Baths.

58 RETURN

Os/C Coys. will forward to Orderly Room by 18.00 on the 20th instant, a list shewing number of men in each Industrial Group as recorded in A.B.64. For example :-

10 men in Group No. 1.
10 men in Group No. 2.
etc. etc.

PART "C."

To The Secretary (Mob. 5d), War Office, Kew, London, S.W.1.

The above-mentioned soldier is suitable for release as a coal-miner and will be employed by .... at ....

Please arrange for his transfer to the Reserve and despatch to the address shown.

....

Date .... *Signature* ....

for Controller of Coal Mines.

PART "D."

To The O.C. Discharge Centre .... Command.

The above-mentioned soldier has been ordered to report to you on .... for transfer to the Reserve for work in a coal mine.

The Deputy Adjutant General, 3rd Echelon, B.E.F., France, has been instructed to despatch to you A.F.s B.103 and 122 and the Officer i/c Records has been ordered to forward to you A.F. B.178 and 120.

The soldier will be transferred to the Reserve and despatched to the address shown in part "C" of this form.

Date ....

Signature, Director of Mobilization.

PART "E."

To .... (firm).

.... (address).

The soldier referred to in Part "A" of this form has been transferred to Class .... of the Reserve.

He has been despatched to you to-day.

Please complete and forward Part "F" of this form as early as possible to the address shown therein.

If at any time the soldier in question should leave your employment, you should immediately report the fact to the Secretary, War Office, Mob. 5d, Kew, London, S.W.1, stating the reasons for which he left your employment.

Date .... *Rank.*

Commanding

.... *Discharge Centre.*

PART "F."

To The Secretary, War Office, Mob. 5d,
Kew, London, S.W. 1.

The soldier referred to in Part "A" of this form reported to me to-day.

Date ....

(Signature, Colliery Firm.)

759 COURT OF ENQUIRY

A Court of Enquiry composed as under will assemble tomorrow at 14.30 at "D" Coy. Officers' Mess to enquire into the absence and loss of kit (if any) of :-

No. 64607 CORPORAL DOBBS W.G. "D" Coy.

PRESIDENT
Captain G.N.WATHEY

MEMBERS
2/Lt.A.B.Yorkston,
2/Lt.J.C.Waterton,

O/C. "D" Company will warn all witnesses to attend.

760 DRESS

Brigade Routine Order No. 500 is repeated for information:-

"During the present cold weather all men will wear Jerkins on all parades, and Officers will wear British Warms or Trench Coats.

Guards will wear Jerkins by day, and greatcoats by night.

761 GUARDS

Brigade Routine Order No. 501 is repeated for information :-

"All Guards will have with them their cleaning material during their tour of duty.

Boots and clothing are at all times to be thoroughly clean".

(signed) J.W.SWANSON Capt. & Adjt.,
15th Battalion K.O.Y.L.I.

P A R T 11

APPOINTMENTS

No. 64109	L/Cpl.	Hope W.A.	"A"	Coy.	To be L/Cpl paid with effect from 3/11/18.
207966	"	Miles G.L.	"A"	"	To be paid L/Cpl with effect from 3/11/18.
39124	"	Blackhall W.	"A"	"	To be L/Cpl paid with effect from 9/10/18
64135	"	Dennis S.	"A"	"	To be L/Cpl paid with effect from 3/11/18.
64131	"	Page F.	"A"	"	To be paid L/Cpl with effect from 9/10/18
64211	"	Nicholson J.	"A"	"	To be paid L/Cpl with effect from 9/10/18.
64113	"	Rason H.	"A"	"	To be paid L/Cpl with effect from 9/10/18.
68317	"	Perelli J.	"A"	"	To be L/Cpl paid with effect from 3/11/18.
68304	"	Simpson W.	"B"	"	To be L/Cpl paid with effect from 15/10/18.
236121	"	Hornsby F.A.	"C"	"	To be paid L/Cpl with effect from 28/5/18.
64427	"	Thacker W.	"C"	"	To be paid L/Cpl with effect from 28/5/18.
64516	"	Lawrence J.	"C"	"	To be paid L/Cpl with effect from 28/8/18.

(To be rendered in triplicate for each man.)

Form A.G. 544/1 (M).

(*a*) Unit .... (*b*)* .... (*c*)* ....

RELEASE FROM THE ARMY FOR COAL-MINING (OVERSEAS).

PART "A."

No. .... Name .... Rank .... Medical Category† ....

Unit .... Corps .... Civil Occupation‡ ....

Name and address of Colliery firm with whom last employed previous to August, 1914 ....

Period of employment with such ....

Home address ....

Mine at which last worked ....

Physical disability (if any) preventing work at his trade† ....

I am willing to be transferred to Class "W" or W(P) of the Army Reserve for the above purpose.

I certify that the above particulars are a true statement of fact.

Date ....

Signature of applicant.

The above particulars have been compared with the entries in Army Book 64, and I am of the opinion that the applicant was a coal-miner employed as such before August 4th, 1914.

....

Signature of O.C. Unit.

TO BE FORWARDED TO THE OFFICER COMMANDING LABOUR GROUP CONCERNED.

NOTE:—These two spaces will be filled in as follows:—
* (*b*) First three letters (in Block Capitals) of name of mine referred to in 2.
* (*c*) Name of mine in full.
e.g. (*b*) AMB.
(*c*) Ambler Thorn.

† To be verified by O.C. Unit.
‡ Insert local term for precise colliery occupation at which you were employed.

PART "B."

To Deputy Adjutant General,
3rd Echelon, G.H.Q.

I have interviewed the above-mentioned man and consider that he fulfills the conditions for release laid down, and that he should be sent home for coal-mining purposes.

Date ....

Interviewing Official.

A duplicate of the form will be forwarded at this stage by the interviewing official to the Controller of Coal Mines, Room 427, Holborn Viaduct Hotel, London, E.C.1, the letters P.M.E. being clearly marked in the left-hand top corner of the envelope.

PRINTED IN FRANCE BY ARMY PRINTING AND STATIONERY SERVICES PRESS A—9/18—7984S—100,000.

76 Q 4600

APPENDIX XIV

Battalion Orders
by
Lieut-Colonel T.W.T.Isaac,
Commanding 15th Battn. King's Own Yorkshire Light Infantry

LOQUOI 19/11/18

Orderly Officer tomorrow.............. 2/Lieut. J.Fox
Next for Duty .... " N.T.Siddle
Company on duty tomorrow .... "D" Company
Next for Duty .... "A" "

762 ROUTINE

Reveille 06.30
Breakfast.......... 07.00
Sick Parade 07.15
Orderly Room 12.00
Dinners............ 12.35
Teas............... 16.30
RETREAT............ 16.30
Lights Out 21.00

763 TRAINING

08.30 - 09.30 Company Commanders Inspecton
09.30 - 10.00 Company Commanders Inspectinn of Billets
10.00 - 11.00 (except "C" Coy) Coy.Commanders parade.
Company Drill and Ceremonial.
Dress - Jerkins

RANGE

The range at G.3.b.7.0. is allotted tomorrow as follows :-
"C" Company - 13.00 - 15.00.
Transport Officer will arrange for a limber to collect two boxes practice S.A.A. from Q.M. Stores to be conveyed to Range by 13.00.

O/C. "C" Company will detail one Subaltern as Range Officer. The Musketry Sergeant will attend the range.

764 MEDICAL PARADES

Medical Parades will be held tomorrow as follows :-

"A" Company	07.30	"C" Company	07.50
"B" "	07.40	"D" "	08.00

Headquarters 08.10

All Officers will arrange direct with the M.O. to "gargle" daily. The R.S.M. will be responsible that all Officers Servants, Cooks, Orderlies etc attend these parades.

765 PROMOTION

The following is extracted from the Supplement to "London Gazette" dated 8th October 1918.

Major T.W.T.ISAAC to be Temp. Lieut-Colonel with effect from 16th April 1918.

766 LEWIS GUNNERS

O/C. Coys. will detail two Lewis Gunners and Coy. L.G. N.C.O. to report to Sergt. Pearson at Battn. Guard Room at 10.00 tomorrow.

767 GUARD MOUNTING

From the 21st instant inclusive the Battn.Guard will be mounted at 08.30 and the Bde. H.Q.Guard at 08.00 hours. The Battn. Orderly Officer will mount both guards.

(To be rendered in triplicate for each man.)

Form A.G. 544/1 (M).

(*a*) Unit .... (*b*)* .... (*c*)* ....

RELEASE FROM THE ARMY FOR COAL-MINING (OVERSEAS).

PART "A."

No. .... Name .... Rank .... Medical Category† ....

Unit .... Corps .... Civil Occupation‡ ....

Name and address of Colliery firm with whom last employed previous to August, 1914 ....

Period of employment with such ....

Home address ....

Mine at which last worked ....

Physical disability (if any) preventing work at his trade† ....

I am willing to be transferred to Class "W" or W(P) of the Army Reserve for the above purpose.

I certify that the above particulars are a true statement of fact.

Date ....

Signature of applicant.

The above particulars have been compared with the entries in Army Book 64, and I am of the opinion that the applicant was a coal-miner employed as such before August 4th, 1914.

....

Signature of O.C. Unit.

TO BE FORWARDED TO THE OFFICER COMMANDING LABOUR GROUP CONCERNED.

NOTE :—These two spaces will be filled in as follows :—

* (*b*) First three letters (in Block Capitals) of name of mine referred to in 2.
* (*c*) Name of mine in full.
e.g. (*b*) AMB.
(*c*) Ambler Thorn.

† To be verified by O.C. Unit.
‡ Insert local term for precise colliery occupation at which you were employed.

PART "B."

To Deputy Adjutant General,
3rd Echelon, G.H.Q.

I have interviewed the above-mentioned man and consider that he fulfills the conditions for release laid down, and that he should be sent home for coal-mining purposes.

Date ....

Interviewing Official.

A duplicate of the form will be forwarded at this stage by the interviewing official to the Controller of Coal Mines, Room 427, Holborn Viaduct Hotel, London, E.C.1, the letters P.M.E. being clearly marked in the left-hand top corner of the envelope.

PRINTED IN FRANCE BY ARMY PRINTING AND STATIONERY SERVICES. PRESS A—9/18—79815—100,000.

768 **LECTURE**

The undermentioned will be detailed by O/C. Coys. to attend a lecture on the work of the British Navy during the War to be given by Commander Spicer-Simpson D.S.O. R.N. at ROUBAIX at 14.30 tomorrow.

One Officer and 8 other ranks per Coy.

This party will parade at the Orderly Room at 13.00 hours. DRESS. Jerkins with belts and sidearms.

Lorries will leave Brigade H.Q. at 13.10.

769 **WAR SERVICE**

Officers Commanding Coys. will forward to Orderly Room by 10.00 hours 21st instant the numbers of men under their Command who enlisted OTHER THAN FOR DURATION OF THE WAR AND HAVE NOT COMPLETED TWO YEARS SERVICE WITH THE COLOURS.

(signed) J.W.SWANSON Capt. & Adjt.,
15th Battalion K.O.Y.L.I.

AFTER ORDER

770 **APPOINTMENTS**

The following appts. are made with effect from today.

2/Lieut. E.Garner	To be Battn.	Sub.Education Officer
Captain P.Fisher	To be Battn.	Sports Officer.

N O T I C E

A competition will be held at 18.00 on the 23rd November at the "Gamecocks" Concert Hall, LANNOY. Entries are invited and prizes will be offerred as follows :-

Best Girl (Appearance and Voice)	50 Francs
Best Comedian	50 "
Best Song or Monologue	50 "
Best Dancer or other Speciality	50 "
Consolation Prize	25 "

O/C. Coys. will forward the names to Orderly Room of all those wishing to enter by 20.00 tomorrow. Facilities will be given for competetors to "make up". Further particulars later.

P A R T I I

APPOINTMENTS & PROMOTIONS

238057	L/Cpl.	Fulton A.	"A" Coy.	To be A/Cpl paid with effect from 19/11/18.
39130	"	Edwards A.	A "	To be A/Cpl (paid) with effect from 19/11/18.
65058 ~~64151~~	"	Neal T.	"A" "	To be paid L/Cpl with effect from 25/7/18
64151	Pte.	Wood J.	"A" "	To be L/Cpl unpaid with effect from 19/11/18

(signed) J.W.SWANSON Capt. & Adjt.
15th Battalion K.O.Y.L.I.

(To be rendered in triplicate for each man.)

Form A.G. 544/1 (M).

(*a*) Unit .... (*b*)* .... (*c*)* ....

RELEASE FROM THE ARMY FOR COAL-MINING (OVERSEAS).

PART "A."

No. .... Name .... Rank .... Medical Category† ....

Unit .... Corps .... Civil Occupation‡ ....

Name and address of Colliery firm with whom last employed previous to August, 1914 ....

Period of employment with such ....

Home address ....

Mine at which last worked ....

Physical disability (if any) preventing work at his trade† ....

I am willing to be transferred to Class "W" or W(P) of the Army Reserve for the above purpose.

I certify that the above particulars are a true statement of fact.

Date ....

Signature of applicant.

The above particulars have been compared with the entries in Army Book 64, and I am of the opinion that the applicant was a coal-miner employed as such before August 4th, 1914.

....

Signature of O.C. Unit.

TO BE FORWARDED TO THE OFFICER COMMANDING LABOUR GROUP CONCERNED.

NOTE:—These two spaces will be filled in as follows:—

* (*b*) First three letters (in Block Capitals) of name of mine referred to in 2.

* (*c*) Name of mine in full.

e.g. (*b*) AMB.

(*c*) Ambler Thorn.

† To be verified by O.C. Unit.

‡ Insert local term for precise colliery occupation at which you were employed.

PART "B."

To Deputy Adjutant General,

3rd Echelon, G.H.Q.

I have interviewed the above-mentioned man and consider that he fulfills the conditions for release laid down, and that he should be sent home for coal-mining purposes.

Date ....

Interviewing Official.

A duplicate of the form will be forwarded at this stage by the interviewing official to the Controller of Coal Mines, Room 427, Holborn Viaduct Hotel, London, E.C.1, the letters P.M.E. being clearly marked in the left-hand top corner of the envelope.

PRINTED IN FRANCE BY ARMY PRINTING AND STATIONERY SERVICES

PRESS A—9/18—7981S—100,000.

Battalion Orders APPENDIX XV
by
Major T.L.Webb
Commanding 15th Battalion King's Own Yorkshire Light Infantry

BUCQUOI 23/11/18.

DETAIL
Orderly Officer tomorrow .... 2/Lieut. W.J.Randles
Next for Duty .... 2/Lieut. A.T.Ogden
Company on duty tomorrow .... "D" Coy.
Next for Duty .... "A" "

788 ROUTINE

Reveille 07.00
Breakfast 07.45
Sick Parade ... 08.00
Dinners .... 12.~~15~~ 30
Teas.......... 16.30
RETREAT....... 16.30
Lights Out 21.00

789 MEDICAL PARADES

Medical Parades will be held tomorrow as follows :-

"A" Coy. 08.15 "C" Coy 08.35
"B" " 08.25 "D" " 08.50
Headquarters 08.55

All Officers will arrange direct with the M.O. to "gargle" daily.

The R.S.M. will be responsible that all Officers Servants, Cooks, Orderlies etc., attend these parades.

790 DIVINE SERVICE

The Battalion will parade tomorrow under Capt.W.E.E.Garrod MC for Divine Service as follows :-

C. of Es. Parade at G.22.b.7.3. (near H.Q.Mess) at 10.00. Right Markers report on ground to R.S.M. at 09.50. DRESS. Drill Order with rifles. The band will attend. Parade will march to the Tannery at G.16.a.8.6. for Service at 11.00 hrs

R.Cs. Parade as above at 11.00. 2/Lieut.E.Garner will march this party to TOUFFLERS CHURCH.

Presbyterians & Non-Conformists. Parade as above at 11.15 hrs. 2/Lieut. S.Dawson will march this party to K.O.S.B. H.Q.

791 OFFICERS- TRANSFER.

T/Lieut. (A/Capt) T.W.HUCKER 15th Battn. East Surrey Regt. (Acting Staff Capt. attd 120th Inf. Bde) is transferred to 15th Battn. K.O.Y.L.I. with effect from 21/7/18 and is posted to "C" Coy. (Authority G.H.Q. No. A.G. 8158/5546 (O) dated 19.11.18.

792 IMMEDIATE AWARD

Under Authority granted by his Majesty the KING, the Field Marshal Commanding-in-Chief has awarded the MILITARY MEDAL to the undermentioned for gallantry in action and devotion to duty :-

No. 64093 Corpl (A/Sgt) R.W.SHAW
King's Own Yorkshire Light Infantry.

792 IMMEDIATE AWARD (contd)

The recipients should be informed at once, and the congratulations of the Divisional and Higher Commanders conveyed to them.

The Commanding Officer also desires to associate himself with the congratulations of the Divl. and Higher Commanders.

793 ANNIVERSARY OF THE BATTLE OF BOURLON WOOD

On 23rd November 1917, the 40th Division with great gallantry attacked and captured BOURLON WOOD and VILLAGE in spite of the enemy's most stubborn resistance.

During the succeeding days the Division repulsed heavy counter attacks delivered in great strength by specially selected enemy troops and fought with remarkable tenacity.

The highest praise was accorded to the Division in the Despatches of the Field Marshal Commanding in Chief, and HIS MAJESTY the KING was graciously pleased to express personally his congratulations to the Divisional Commander shortly after the battle.

The Oak-leaves and acorn were added to the Divisional sign in commemoration of the occasion.

794 PASSES

25%

Reference Battn. Order 727, passes to leave the billeting Area may be granted up to 22.00 by Coy. Commanders.

Passes for Private soldiers may be signed direct by the Coy. Commanders. Passes for N.C.Os. will be sent to the R.S.M. by Coy. Orderly Sergts. by 12.00 daily.

All N.C.Os. and men on return to Battalion Billeting Area will hand in their passes to the N.C.O. i/c Guard.

P A R T 11

APPOINTMENTS

No. 64524 L/Cpl. Tamkin W. "C" Coy. Apptd paid L/Cpl with effect from 25/7/18.

(signed) J.W.SWANSON Capt. & Adjt.,
25/11/18. 15th Battalion K.O.Y.L.I.

N O T I C E

SPORTS

The following Inter Coy. Football Match will take place tomorrow at 14.00 on Parade Ground at G.24.b.1.8.

"A" & "B" Coys -v- "D" Coy.

APPENDIX XVI

Battalion Orders
by
Lieut-Colonel T.W.T.Isaac,
Commanding 15th Battalion King's Own Yorkshire Light Infantry

TOUFFLERS

DETAIL 26/11/18.

Orderly Officer tomorrow............. 2/Lieut A.MacTavish
Next for duty .... 2/Lieut W.A.Patterson
Company on duty tomorrow .... "D" Company
Next for Duty......................... "A" Company

810 ROUTINE

Reveille....... 06.30
ROUSE PARADE... 07.00
Breakfast...... 07.00
Sick Parade.... 07.15
Orderly Room... 12.00
Dinners........ 12.30
Tea............ 16.30
RETREAT........ 16.30
Lights Out..... 21.00

811 TRAINING

Special parades - The undermentioned Special Parades will be held tomorrow at G.24.b.1.8. at times stated below :- Dress - Jerkins and as detailed separately, to-day :-

09.30 "B" Coy. Commanding Officer's ~~Parade~~ Inspection
10.00 "A" " Commanding Officer's Inspection
10.30 "A" " G.O.Cs. Inspection

The band will attend the 10.30 parade.

09.00 - 10.00 "C" & "D" Coys on Coy. Parade Ground Coy. Commander's Inspection
10.00 - 11.00 "C" & "D" Coys. Coy. Drill & Coy. Ceremonial.

Except as stated above Coys. will be at the disposal of Coy. Commander's tomorrow for cleaning up etc

812 EDUCATION

Drawing and Designing Class.- The undermentioned will attend above Class in Schoolroom of Cameron High. NECHIN at 17.00 each Monday, Wednesday and Friday.

No. 64293 Pte.Hitchen W. "B" Coy.) attd.
64247 " Bowring A. "B" Coy.) Bn. H.Q.

813 OFFICERS

The undermentioned Officers are attached from 11th Battalion Cameron Highlanders for "temporary" duty, and are posted to Coys. as under. Batmen brought by these Officers will be sent back to join their Battn. immediately. O/C. Coys. will provide Batmen for these Officers.

Lieut. A.Miller "D" Company.
2/Lt. H.C.Nichols "B" "
" W.A.Patterson "D" "
" A.Mactavish "D" "

3

if agreeable: the Brigade Major of 121 Bde has told Col Maitland to ask for these as he handed all his to 40th Division on previous relief.

Colin Smee
Capt.
20th Middlesex Regt
Liaison Officer to 121 Bde.

92

814 COMPANY ORDERLY OFFICER

O/C Coys. will detail daily a Coy. Orderly Officer and will forward the name of the Officer to Orderly Room by 09.00 daily. This Officer will attend Rouse Parade and Coy. Dinners, and will not leave the Battalion Billeting Area without permission of the Adjutant. The Coy. Orderly Officer will attend all G.O.Cs. inspections.

815 ROUSE PARADE

A Roll Call will be held at Rouse Parade daily and will be attended by the Coy. Orderly Officer.

816 EDUCATION CLASSES

Reference returned received to-day from Coys. re illiterate men, these men will be ordered to attend the "3 Rs" Class at the times laid down in Battalion Order 802. They will report tomorrow morning at Orderly Room to Sergt Pearson at 08.30. Men attending this Class will be excused ALL PARADES.

817 PARADE STATE

O/C "A" Coy. will render to Orderly Room by 09.00 tomorrow a parade state as detailed in the orders issued separately today, shewing numbers by ranks.

818 COMMAND

Lieut-Colonel T.W.T.Isaac assumes Command of the Battn. 25/11/18 (from Bde. H.Q.)

(signed) J.W.SWANSON Capt & Adjt.,
15th Battalion K.O.Y.L.I.

26/11/18

N O T I C E.

PROBABLES

Cpl Knight "C" Co.
Lingard "D" Co. RQMS. Miles
Sgt. Scougall "C" Co. Denny "A" Co Warner "B" Co.
Walker "D" Co. Murdie "D" Co. Slater "D" Co. Pope "D" Co.
Pryor "D" Co.

Wright "A" Co.
Sharp "B" Co. Bevan "B" Co. L/C. Plackhall "A"
Cpl. Stow "B" Co. Moores "C" Co. Wilkinson "B" Co.
Haywood "D" Co. Ripley "D" Co Keeby "A" Co.
McCall "D" Co.

Referee:- Pte. Pilkington "B" Co.

To be played on ground behind "A" Cos. billets at 14.00

If any of the above men are unable to play they must report to their Coy. Sports Representative before 09.00 tomorrow the 27th inst. who will advise Capt. Fisher immediately.

66

7+ 8 pages

CONFIDENTIAL.

WAR DIARY

of

15th Bn K.O.Y.L.I.

for the month of

DECEMBER

1918.

8R 7

Miss Russell

VOLUME VII

SECRET

Volume VII

Instructions regarding War Diaries and Intelligence Summaries are contained in F. S. Regs., Part II. and the Staff Manual respectively. Title pages will be prepared in manuscript.

December 1918

WAR DIARY
or
INTELLIGENCE SUMMARY.
(Erase heading not required.)

Army Form C. 2118.

15th Bn K.O.Y.L.I.

Page 1.

Place	Date	Hour	Summary of Events and Information	Remarks and references to Appendices
			Divine Service under Captain WATNEY 10.40. 2nd Lieut J. F. EVANS	Mw
TOUFFLERS	1/12/18		appointed Sub education officer vice 2nd Lieut E. GARNER Football	Mw
			The Battalion played Brigade H.Q. on the Brigade ground. The Battalion won 6-2	Mw
	2/12/18		Training under Company Commanders The G.O.C. inspected C Company.	Mw
	3/12/18		Training under Company Commanders Boxing Tournament held at	Mw
			Roubaix. Battalion Cross Country Run in the afternoon	Mw
	4/12/18		Inspection by the G.O.C. Division cancelled. Training under Company	Mw
			Commanders. Riding school for officers started	Mw
	5/12/18		Training under Company Commanders.	Mw
	6/12/18		Baths allotted to the Battalion at Sannoy. Croix de Guerre (Division	Mw
			with Silver Star) awarded to No 84171 Sergeant L HANSON (authority	Mw
			D.R.O. 2506 dated 6/12/18)	Mw

D. D. & L., London, E.C.
(10340) Wt W5300/P713 750,000 3/18 E 2688 Forms/C2118/19.

Volume VII

Instructions regarding War Diaries and Intelligence Summaries are contained in F. S. Regs., Part II. and the Staff Manual respectively. Title pages will be prepared in manuscript.

December 1918

WAR DIARY
or
INTELLIGENCE SUMMARY.
(Erase heading not required.)

Army Form C. 2118.

15th Bn K.O.Y.L.I. Page 2

Place	Date	Hour	Summary of Events and Information	Remarks and references to Appendices
			His Majesty The KING visited Toufflers. Lt Colonel T.W.T. ISAACS commanded	MW
Toufflers	7 12/18		a group of 1600 men who were divided into groups along the road to	MW
			welcome the King. A Regimental Christmas Dinner and Finance Committee	MW
			were appointed.	MW
			Divine Service 10.20 The G.O.C Division presented the following Medals in	MW
	8 12/18		the Square Lannoy at 14.30	MW
			Captain W.E.E. GARROD. MC — Bar to MC	MW
			2nd Lieut S. SCARR — MC	MW
			No 6008 A/CSM ROBERTS — M.M. and Bar	MW
			No 64092 A/Sgt SHAW R.W. — M.M	MW
			No 64626 Pte BROADLEY. B — M.M	MW
			No 64588 " BRAZIER. J — M.M.	MW
			No 64171 Sgt HANSON L. — Croix de Guerre with Silver Star.	MW
	9 12/18		Training Company Route Marches. The G.O.C inspected A Company. Lecture	MW
			on Settlement of Soldiers on the Land at Roubaix.	MW
			Brigade inspected by the G.O.C. Division Lt Col T.W.T. ISAAC in Command	MW
	10 12/18		of the Brigade Captain R. FISHER in Command of the Battalion.	MW

D. D. & L., London, E.C.
(10340) Wt W5300/P713 750,000 3/18 & 2688 Forms/C2118/13.

Volume VII

Instructions regarding War Diaries and Intelligence Summaries are contained in F. S. Regs., Part II. and the Staff Manual respectively. Title pages will be prepared in manuscript.

December 1918

WAR DIARY
or
INTELLIGENCE SUMMARY.
(Erase heading not required.)

Army Form C. 2118.

15th Bn K.O.Y.L.I.

Page 3

Place	Date	Hour	Summary of Events and Information	Remarks and references to Appendices
TOUFFLERS	11.12.18		Training under Company Commanders. Board of Survey met to check the Battalion Stores.	JW JW
	12.12.18		Training under Company Commanders. The G.O.C. inspected the Battalion Billets	JW
	13.12.18		Training under Company Commanders. The G.O.C. inspected D. Company. Lecture at Lannoy by the Revd G.A.S. KENNEDY on "Demobilization". Platoon Rifle Competition one platoon from each Company take part. Captain J.W. SWANSON appointed Adjutant of the Battalion. A second recreation room for A & C Companies opened opposite C Companies billet.	JW JW JW JW JW
	14.12.18		Training. Divisional Ceremonial Parade. Lecture at Roubaix on the "British Empire"	JW JW
	15.12.18		Training under Company Commanders. Adjutants parade in the afternoon three times a week commenced	JW JW
	16.12.18		Training under Company Commanders	JW
	17.12.18		Training. Divisional Ceremonial Parade. Lending Library started in Battalion Recreation Room.	JW JW

(10340) Wt W5300/P713 750,000 3/18 S 2688 Forms/C2118/15. D. D. & L., London, E.C.

Volume VII

Instructions regarding War Diaries and Intelligence Summaries are contained in F. S. Regs., Part II. and the Staff Manual respectively. Title pages will be prepared in manuscript.

December 1918

WAR DIARY
or
INTELLIGENCE SUMMARY.
(Erase heading not required.)

Army Form C. 2118.

Page 4.

15th Bn K.O.Y.L.I.

Place	Date	Hour	Summary of Events and Information	Remarks and references to Appendices
Touffiers	18/12/18		Training under Company Commanders. Brigade Cinematograph opens at Lannoy	MW
	19/12/18		Training Company Route Marches	MW
	20/12/18		Training under Company Commanders. Skating Rink at Roubaix reserved for officers 5:30 pm – 7 pm two afternoons a week	MW
	21/12/18		Training under Company Commanders. One Platoon per Company practice on the Range for A.R.A. Competition	MW
	22/12/18		Divine Service 10.00	MW
	23/12/18		Training under Company Commanders.	MW
	24/12/18		Training under Company Commanders. The afternoon fully occupied with the issuing of Xmas fare and decorating the mess Quarters	MW
	25/12/18		Xmas Day Divine Service in the Concert Hall at 10.30. The Commanding Officer & Staff visited all the mess dinners Commencing	MW

D. D. & L., London, E.C.
(20340) Wt W5300/P713 750,000 3/18 Sch. 2688 Forms/C2118/15.

Volume VII

December 1918

Instructions regarding War Diaries and Intelligence Summaries are contained in F. S. Regs., Part II. and the Staff Manual respectively. Title pages will be prepared in manuscript.

WAR DIARY
or
INTELLIGENCE SUMMARY.
(Erase heading not required.)

15th Bn K.O.Y.L.I.

Army Form C. 2118.

Page 5

Place	Date	Hour	Summary of Events and Information	Remarks and references to Appendices
TOURNAI	25th		1230 Each Company dining in its own dining hall for the first time	[initials]
			The dinners were a great success. The Pioneers had by means of	[initials]
			very good work been able to provide all Companies with sufficient	[initials]
			tables & forms to seat every man. plates etc had been procured	[initials]
			and all the rooms were splendidly decorated by Companies. The	[initials]
			Commanding Officer received an enthusiastic reception from every	[initials]
			Company. The mens dinners consisted of fresh pork apple sauce	[initials]
			vegetables plum pudding prunes & custard nuts & beer. A Concert	[initials]
			was given in the evening by the Battalion Concert party (The Acorns)	[initials]
			and was a great success. the Concert Hall was full about 400	[initials]
			men being present	[initials]
	26th		Training under Company Commanders. Lieut Col T.W.T. ISAAC	[initials]

D. D. & L., London, E.C.
(10340) Wt W5300/P713 750,000 3/18 E 2688 Forms/C2118/15.

Volume VII

December 1918

Army Form C. 2118.

Page 6

WAR DIARY
or
INTELLIGENCE SUMMARY.
(Erase heading not required.)

Instructions regarding War Diaries and Intelligence Summaries are contained in F. S. Regs., Part II. and the Staff Manual respectively. Title pages will be prepared in manuscript.

15th Bn K.O.Y.L.I.

Place	Date	Hour	Summary of Events and Information	Remarks and references to Appendices
Toufflers	26/12/18		assumed command of the 120th Infantry Brigade during the temporary absence of the Brigadier General. MAJOR T L WEBB assumed command of the Battalion. Football. The Battalion team v 23rd Lancashire Fusiliers. Battalion won 3-0. All Officers were entertained to dinner in H Q Mess	MW
	27/12/18		Training under Company Commanders. The Battalion was marched in the afternoon to the Brigade Cinema Hall which had been taken by the Battalion for the afternoon. The performance was much enjoyed	MW
	28/12/18		Training under Company Commanders. The Baths at Lannoy were allotted to the Battalion	MW
	29/12/18		Divine Service in Concert Hall at 9.30. The Battalion Concert Party gave a Concert to the Children of TOUFFLERS in the afternoon	MW

D. D. & L., London, E.C.
(10340) Wt W5300/P713 750,000 3/18 Sch. 2688 Forms/C2118/15.

Volume VII

Instructions regarding War Diaries and Intelligence Summaries are contained in F. S. Regs., Part II. and the Staff Manual respectively. Title pages will be prepared in manuscript.

December 1918

WAR DIARY
or
INTELLIGENCE SUMMARY.
(Erase heading not required.)

Army Form C. 2118.

Page 7.

15th Bn K.O.Y.L.I.

Place	Date	Hour	Summary of Events and Information	Remarks and references to Appendices
TOUFFLERS	29th 12 Contd		and to the Civilian population in the evening both performances were	[illegible]
			well attended and appeared to be much enjoyed	[illegible]
	30th 12		Training under Company Commanders	[illegible]
	31st 12		Training under Company Commanders	[illegible]

[illegible] Lt Col
Cmdg 15th Bn K.O.Y.L.I.

D. D. & L., London, E.C.
(10340) Wt W5300/P713 750,000 3/18 Sch. 52a Forms/C2118/15.

~~Confidential~~ 40

#8

WAR DIARY F.H. Vol 8

OF

15th Bn K O Y L.I

FOR

JANUARY 1919

VOLUME VIII

Commdg 15th Bn K.O.Y.L.I. Major

Secret

Volume VIII

January 1919
15th K.O.Y.L.I.

Army Form C. 2118.

WAR DIARY
or
INTELLIGENCE SUMMARY.
(Erase heading not required.)

Page I

Instructions regarding War Diaries and Intelligence Summaries are contained in F. S. Regs., Part II. and the Staff Manual respectively. Title pages will be prepared in manuscript.

Place	Date	Hour	Summary of Events and Information	Remarks and references to Appendices
TOUTTIERS	1/1/19		Lieut Colonel T.W.T. ISAAC resumed command of the Battalion	MW
			Major L.M. SANDISON rejoined from Senior Officers Course Aldershot	MW
			Training under Company Commanders.	MW
	2/1/19		Training Battalion Route March. The G.O.C. Brigade inspected	MW
			the Battalion billets. Afternoon Brigade Rugby football practice	MW
			match	MW
	3/1/19		Training under Company Commanders and Baths at Vaurey	MW
			Afternoon Rugby football match. Brigade team v Divisional	MW
			Troops. Divisional Troops won.	MW
	4/1/19		The G.O.C. Division inspected the Battalion. He expressed	MW
			himself as highly satisfied with everything he saw, and ordered	MW
			the following to be read out to all ranks on parade	MW
			"The Divisional Commander has expressed himself as highly	MW

Volume VIII

January 1919
15th Bn K.O.Y.L.I.

WAR DIARY
or
INTELLIGENCE SUMMARY.
(Erase heading not required.)

Army Form C. 2118.

Page 11

Instructions regarding War Diaries and Intelligence Summaries are contained in F. S. Regs., Part II. and the Staff Manual respectively. Title pages will be prepared in manuscript.

Place	Date	Hour	Summary of Events and Information	Remarks and references to Appendices
Toufflers	4/1/19 (Contd)		Satisfied with all he saw today, the drill, turnout and appearance of the troops gave him every gratification, as also did the condition of the billets which he inspected." Special order of the day by the G.O.C. 120th Infantry Brigade was published as follows:—	MW
			535 Special order	Appendix I
			"The Brigadier wishes to congratulate all ranks of the 15th Battalion K.O.Y.L.I. on the first rate appearance of the Battalion at the Major-General's Inspection this morning. The Brigadier has seldom seen a better turned out Battalion even at home. This excellent result can only have been attained after an immense amount of both hard & willing work on the part of all concerned. The Major-General was extremely pleased with all he saw, and informed the Brigadier that he considered the 15th Bn K.O.Y.L.I. the best Battalion in the Division" (Copy attached)	MW

D. D. & L., London, E.C.
(10340) W1 W5300/P713 750,000 3/18 Sch. 2688 Forms/C2118/15.

Volume VIII

Instructions regarding War Diaries and Intelligence Summaries are contained in F. S. Regs., Part II. and the Staff Manual respectively. Title pages will be prepared in manuscript.

January 1919
15th Bn K.O.Y.L.I.

WAR DIARY
or
INTELLIGENCE SUMMARY.
(Erase heading not required.)

Army Form C. 2118.

Page 111

Place	Date	Hour	Summary of Events and Information	Remarks and references to Appendices
Touffiers	5/1/19		Divine Service in Concert Hall at 9.30. The Battalion Concert party gave a concert for the civilians at 6 pm	Mr
	6/1/19		Training under Company Commanders	Mr
	7/1/19		Major L.M. SANDISON took over command of the Battalion during the absence on leave to the U.K. of Lt Colonel T.W.T. ISAAC. Battalion parade 9.30. The Battalion practiced marching in slow time preparatory to presentation of Colours	Mr
	8/1/19		Training under Company Commanders	Mr
	9/1/19		Training under Company Commanders	Mr
	10/1/19		Brigade Ceremonial parade for Consecration & Reception of Colours (practice) Afternoon football. Bn team v 17th Warwick Regt. ended in a draw	Mr

D. D. & L., London, E.C.
(10340) Wt W5300/P713 750,000 3/18 S 2688 Forms/C2118/15.

Volume VIII

January 1919
15th Bn K.O.Y.L.I.

WAR DIARY
or
INTELLIGENCE SUMMARY.
(*Erase heading not required.*)

Army Form C. 2118.

Page IV

Instructions regarding War Diaries and Intelligence Summaries are contained in F. S. Regs., Part II. and the Staff Manual respectively. Title pages will be prepared in manuscript.

Place	Date	Hour	Summary of Events and Information	Remarks and references to Appendices
Touffleurs	11/1/19		Brigade Ceremonial parade (practice) The Commanding Officer inspected all Regimental Institutes & Workshops	MW
	12/1/19		Divine Service in Concert Hall 10.45. The Bn Concert party gave a concert open to Civilians at 6 pm	MW
	13/1/19		Brigade Ceremonial parade (practice). Baths allotted to the Battalion at Lannoy. Football in the afternoon The Battalion v 17th Worcestershire Rgt (Re-play) result the Battalion lost 3-1	MW
	14/1/19		Brigade Ceremonial practice for No 1 Guard. Football in the afternoon between platoon teams.	MW
	15/1/19		Brigade Ceremonial practice	MW
	16/1/19		Brigade Ceremonial practice for No I Guard. The Officers Club Roubaix opened with a Concert by the Lena Ashwell Concert party	MW

D. D. & L., London, E.C.
(10340) Wt W5300/P713 750,000 3/18 & 2688 Forms/C2118/15.

Volume VIII

Instructions regarding War Diaries and Intelligence Summaries are contained in F. S. Regs., Part II. and the Staff Manual respectively. Title pages will be prepared in manuscript.

January 1919
15th Bn K.O.Y.L.I.

WAR DIARY
or
INTELLIGENCE SUMMARY.
(Erase heading not required.)

Army Form C. 2118.

Page V

Place	Date	Hour	Summary of Events and Information	Remarks and references to Appendices
TOUFFLERS	16/1/19	(Contd)	in the afternoon and a Concert by the 15th Bn K.O.Y.L.I. Concert	Mr
			party (The Acorns) in the evening.	Mr
			Brigade Ceremonial practice. Football in the afternoon. platoon	Mr
	17/1/19			Mr
			competitions.	
				Mr
	18/1/19		Brigade Ceremonial practice	
			Divine Service in Concert Hall at 10.30. A Concert open to	Mr
	19/1/19			Mr
			Civilians given by the Bn Concert party in Concert Hall at 18.00.	
			Presentation of Colours to all Battalions of the 120 Brigade in	Mr
	20/1/19		the Square at G.2.c.9.6. at 10.30. The Colours were presented	Mr
			by the Corps Commander. The Battalion were represented as follows	Mr
			No I Guard composed of 2 Sgts and 20 other ranks per Battalion	Mr
			under the command of Major T.L. WEBB.	Mr
			No IV Guard Captain LINDEMERE, 2nd Lieut SCARR M.C. & WATERTON	Mr

D. D. & L., London, E.C.
(10340) Wt W5300/P713 750,000 3/18 2688 Forms/C2118/15.

Volume VIII

January 1919
15th Bn K.O.Y.L.I.

WAR DIARY *or* **INTELLIGENCE SUMMARY.**
(Erase heading not required.)

Army Form C. 2118.

Page VI

Instructions regarding War Diaries and Intelligence Summaries are contained in F. S. Regs., Part II. and the Staff Manual respectively. Title pages will be prepared in manuscript.

Place	Date	Hour	Summary of Events and Information	Remarks and references to Appendices
			—	Mw
Touffiers	20/1/19	(Contd)	+ 60 NCOs + men of the Battalion. CSM ARMSTRONG	Mw
			Battalion Colour party Lieut N. GYE.	Mw
			and Sgt ADAMS.	
			The following Brigade Order was published	Mw
			"The Brigadier wishes to congratulate all Ranks on the	Mw
			appearance of the Brigade on to-days parade for Presentation and	Mw
			Trooping of the Colours. The Corps Commander expressed himself	Mw
			as highly pleased with all he saw and wished all ranks	Mw
			to be informed that he thoroughly appreciated and realized	Mw
			the keeness and hard work necessary to produce so excellent	Mw
			a result	Mw
	21/1/19		Battalion attended Baths at Lannoy	Mw
	22/1/19		Training under Company Commanders. The Commanding Officer lectured the Battalion on "The necessity for a Post Bellum Army"	Mw

D. D. & L., London, E.C.
(10340) Wt W5300/P713 750,000 3/18 E 2688 Forms/C2118/15.

Volume VIII

Instructions regarding War Diaries and Intelligence Summaries are contained in F. S. Regs., Part II. and the Staff Manual respectively. Title pages will be prepared in manuscript.

January 1919
15th Bn K.O.Y.L.I.

WAR DIARY
or
INTELLIGENCE SUMMARY.
(Erase heading not required.)

Army Form C. 2118.

Page VII

Place	Date	Hour	Summary of Events and Information	Remarks and references to Appendices
TOUFFLERS	23/1/19		Lt Col T.W.T. ISAAC resumed command of the Battalion from leave.	MW
			Training under Company Commanders. The Battalion Concert party	MW
			performed in the "Gamecocks Hall" Sannoy at 17.30	MW
	24/1/19		Training Battalion Route March lasting 2 hours	MW
	25/1/19		Kit & billet inspections. The Commanding Officer inspected B Company	MW
			in full marching order	MW
	26/1/19		Divine Service in the Concert Hall at 10.30. Concert by the Battalion	MW
			Concert party open to Civilians in the Concert Hall at 18.00	MW
	27/1/19		Owing to fall of snow training restricted to a Battalion parade	MW
			for P.T. & B.F. Lecture by MAJOR. L.M. SANDISON. on "The	MW
			advantages of the Post Bellum Army"	MW
	28/1/19		Training all Companies "Dog & Stick" parade	MW

Volume VIII

Instructions regarding War Diaries and Intelligence Summaries are contained in F. S. Regs., Part II. and the Staff Manual respectively. Title pages will be prepared in manuscript.

January 1919
15th Bn K.O.Y.L.I.

WAR DIARY
or
INTELLIGENCE SUMMARY.
(Erase heading not required.)

Army Form C. 2118.

Page VIII

Place	Date	Hour	Summary of Events and Information	Remarks and references to Appendices
TOUFFLERS	29/1/19		The Battalion attended baths at Lannoy	MW
	30/1/19		Lt Col T.W.T. ISAAC assumed Command of the 120th Brigade	MW
			during the temporary absence on leave of the Brigade Commander	MW
			MAJOR L.M. SANDISON assumed Command of the Battalion	MW
			Training Battalion "Rendezvous March"	MW
	31/1/19		Training Battalion parade for PT & BF. Lecture by Company	MW
			Commanders	MW
			Number demobilised during month of January – 5 Officers 254 Other ranks.	

1/2/19

L.M. Sandison Major
Commdg 15th Bn. K.O.Y.L.I.

D. D. & L., London, E.C.
(10340) Wt W5300/P713 750,000 3/18 S 2688 Forms/C2118/15.

COPY

No. [illegible]

BRIGADE ROUTINE ORDERS

by

Brigadier General The Hon. W.P.HORE RUTHVEN, C.M.G. D.S.O.,

Commanding 120th Infantry Brigade.

4th January 1919.

53[illegible] SPECIAL ORDER

THE BRIGADIER WISHES TO CONGRATULATE ALL RANKS OF THE 15TH BATTALION K.O.Y.L.I. ON THE FIRST RATE APPEARANCE OF THE BATTALION AT THE MAJOR-GENERAL'S INSPECTION THIS MORNING. THE BRIGADIER HAS SELDOM SEEN A BETTER TURNED-OUT BATTALION EVEN AT HOME. THIS EXCELLENT RESULT CAN ONLY HAVE BEEN ATTAINED AFTER AN IMMENSE AMOUNT OF BOTH HARD AND WILLING WORK ON THE PART OF ALL CONCERNED. THE MAJOR-GENERAL WAS EXTREMELY PLEASED WITH ALL HE SAW AND INFORMED THE BRIGADIER THAT HE CONSIDERED THE 15TH BATTALION K. O. Y. L. I. THE BEST BATTALION IN THE DIVISION.

(signed) W.P.Hore Ruthven Brigadier-General,
Commanding 120th Infantry Brigade.

APPENDIX

CONFIDENTIAL

WAR DIARY

FOR THE MONTH OF

FEBRUARY 1919

of

15th Bn KOYLI

789

VOLUME IX

SECRET

T. W. T. Isaac. Lieut: Colonel
Commanding 1st Bn K.O.Y.L.I.

Volume IX

February 1919
15th Bn K.O.Y.L.I.

Army Form C. 2118.

WAR DIARY
or
INTELLIGENCE SUMMARY.
(Erase heading not required.)

Instructions regarding War Diaries and Intelligence Summaries are contained in F. S. Regs., Part II. and the Staff Manual respectively. Title pages will be prepared in manuscript.

Page 1

Place	Date	Hour	Summary of Events and Information	Remarks and references to Appendices
TOUFFLERS	Feb 1919 1st		Inspection of billets & Regimental Institutes by the Commanding Officer. The Battalion Concert Party gave a performance at 20.30 hours in the Officers Club Roubaix. Demobilization has much depleted the Strength of the Battalion. 20 men were demobilized today.	MW
	2nd		Divine Service in Concert Hall at 11.00 hours. The Sermon was preached by The Revd N. TALBOT. M.C. Assistant Chaplain General 5th Army.	MW
	3rd		Training. Battalion Route March.	MW
	4th		Training under Company Commanders. Battalion attended baths at Roubaix.	MW
	5th		Training "Dog & Stick" parade. The Battalion Concert party gave a performance in Concert Hall at 18.30 hours.	MW
	6th		Training under Company Commanders. 2nd Lieut G. BROWN. left the Battalion for demobilization.	MW

D. D. & L., London, E.C.
(10340) Wt W5300/P713 750,000 3/18 Sch. 2688 Forms/C2118/15.

Volume IX

February 1919
15th Bn K.O.Y.L.I.

Army Form C. 2118.

Instructions regarding War Diaries and Intelligence Summaries are contained in F. S. Regs., Part II. and the Staff Manual respectively. Title pages will be prepared in manuscript.

WAR DIARY
or
INTELLIGENCE SUMMARY.
(Erase heading not required.)

Page 2.

Place	Date	Hour	Summary of Events and Information	Remarks and references to Appendices
TOUFFLERS	1919 Feb 7th		A & C Companies were amalgamated, owing to the decreased strength of the Battalion.	MW
	8th		B & D Companies amalgamated. A & C Companies now known as No 1 Company under the Command of Capt. P FISHER. B & D Companies as No. 2. Company under Command of Capt. LINDERMERE. 2nd Lieuts J. BOTCHERBY & J.C. WATERTON, left the Battalion for demobilization.	MW
	9th		Divine Service in Concert Hall at 10.30 hours. Farewell concert given by Battalion Concert party in Concert Hall at 18.15 hours. Captain G.N. WATNEY left the Battalion for demobilization.	MW
	10th		Training under Company Commanders. 27 men were demobilized.	MW
	11th		Training under Company Commanders	MW
	12th		Training under Company Commanders. Baths at Roubaix	MW

D. D. & L., London, E.C.
(10340) Wt W5300/P713 750,000 3/18 S 2688 Forms/C2118/15.

Volume IX

Instructions regarding War Diaries and Intelligence Summaries are contained in F. S. Regs., Part II. and the Staff Manual respectively. Title pages will be prepared in manuscript.

February 1919
15th Bn K.O.Y.L.I.

WAR DIARY
or
INTELLIGENCE SUMMARY.
(Erase heading not required.)

Army Form C. 2118.

Page 3

Place	Date	Hour	Summary of Events and Information	Remarks and references to Appendices
TOUFFLERS	1919 Feb. 13th		Training under Company Commanders. Extract from Supplement to London Gazette "Temp Sec. Lt. to be Temp Lt. J.F. EVANS (27.11.18)" 59 men of the Battalion proceeded for Demobilization.	MW
	14th		Training under Company Commanders. 42 men proceeded for Demobilization	MW
	15th		Training under Company Commanders. 20 men proceeded for Demobilization	MW
	16th		Sunday but no Church Parade held owing to low strength to which Battalion had fallen.	MW
	17th		Training under Company Commanders. Lieut-Colonel T.W.T. ISAAC resumed Command of the Battalion. 2nd Lieut N.C. MOORE left the Battalion for Demobilization	MW
	18th		Training under Company Commanders	MW
	19th		Training under Company Commanders	MW

D. D. & L., London, E.C.
(10340) Wt W5300/P713 750,000 3/18 ≤ 2688 Forms/C2118/15.

Volume IX

Instructions regarding War Diaries and Intelligence Summaries are contained in F. S. Regs., Part II. and the Staff Manual respectively. Title pages will be prepared in manuscript.

February 1919
15th Bn K.O.Y.L.I.

WAR DIARY
or
INTELLIGENCE SUMMARY.
(Erase heading not required.)

Army Form C. 2118.

Page 4.

Place	Date	Hour	Summary of Events and Information	Remarks and references to Appendices
TOUFFLERS	Feb 20th		Training under Company Commanders. Battalion attended baths at Roubaix	
	21st		Training under Company Commanders.	
	22nd		Ditto Ditto	
	23rd		Sunday Holy Communion in Concert Hall at 10.15. MAJOR L. M. SANDISON left the Battalion for a Course on Lecturing in England	
	24th		Training under Company Commanders.	
	25th		Ditto Ditto	
	26th		Ditto Ditto	
	27th		Ditto Ditto. Adjutant's Parade for Subaltern Officers at 10.15	
	28th		Ditto Ditto Tactical exercise carried out by Officers of No 2 Company. The weather during the month of February has	

D. D. & L., London, E.C.
(10,140) Wt W5300/P713 750,000 3/18 & 2688 Forms/C2118/15.

Volume IX

Instructions regarding War Diaries and Intelligence Summaries are contained in F. S. Regs., Part II. and the Staff Manual respectively. Title pages will be prepared in manuscript.

February 1919

15th Bn K.O.Y.L.I.

WAR DIARY
or
INTELLIGENCE SUMMARY.
(Erase heading not required.)

Army Form C. 2118.

Page 5

Place	Date	Hour	Summary of Events and Information	Remarks and references to Appendices
Toufflers	Feb 28th (Contd)		been so bad, that all outdoor sport has been impossible. football	Mr
			was arranged for the afternoon of the 27th but had to be cancelled	Mr
			owing to the State of the ground	Mr
			Total strength of the Battalion at the end of February.	Mr
			25 Officers 228 other ranks.	Mr
			Total numbers of those still serving with the Battalion who	Mr
			joined the Battalion on its formation at BUYSCHEURRE	Mr
			on the 10th June 1918.	Mr
			2 Officers (CAPT. J.W. SWANSON, Adjutant and Lieut	Mr
			& 2nd Lt F. NUNLEY)	Mr
			137 other ranks	Mr

T.W.T. [signature] Lieut.-Col,
Commdg. 15th Bn K.O.Y.L.I.

D. D. & L., London, E.C.
(10340) Wt W5300/P713 750,000 3/18 Sch. 2688 Forms/C2118/15.

10A

3 sheets

D. A. G.

British Troops in France.

Herewith please final War Diary for the unit under my Command.

Pontefract
1. 6. 19

W. B. Jolly Capt & Adj
for Lieut.-Col. Cmdg 15th K.O.Y.L.I.

Volume XII

15th Bn KOYLI

May 1919

Instructions regarding War Diaries and Intelligence Summaries are contained in F. S. Regs., Part II. and the Staff Manual respectively. Title pages will be prepared in manuscript.

WAR DIARY
or
INTELLIGENCE SUMMARY.
(Erase heading not required.)

May – June

Army Form C. 2118.

VS 12913

Page 1

Place	Date	Hour	Summary of Events and Information	Remarks and references to Appendices
Croix	1919 May 1st	—	Troops confined to billets – To keep clear of any French Political meetings or processions	Jm
	2nd	–	Routine as usual	Jm
	3rd	–	—"—	Jm
	4th	–	Divine Service in English Church –	Jm
	5th	–	Routine as usual	Jm
	6th	—	1 Officer & 2 men proceeded on a two days pleasure trip to Ostend: ZEEBRUGGE & BRUGES	Jm
	7th	—	Routine as usual.	Jm
	8th	—	10 Other ranks proceeded to join 83rd Prisoners of War Coy at ARQUES. Struck off strength of Battalion & posted to KOYLI Detail Bn	Jm
			Divisional Cadre Group Sports held at Croix. A large number of the Cadre of the Battn competed.	Jm
	9th	–	Routine as usual	Jm
	10th	—	9 Other ranks proceeded to join 83rd Prisoners of War Coy at ARQUES. Struck off strength of Battalion & posted to KOYLI Detail Bn	Jm
	11th		Divine Service in English Church Croix	Jm

D. D. & L., London, E.C. (10340) Wt W5300/P713 750,000 3/18 Sch. 2688 Forms/C2118/15.

15th Bn K.O.Y.L.I.

Volume XII

Instructions regarding War Diaries and Intelligence Summaries are contained in F. S. Regs., Part II. and the Staff Manual respectively. Title pages will be prepared in manuscript.

WAR DIARY
or
INTELLIGENCE SUMMARY.
(Erase heading not required.)

May 1919 + June

Army Form C. 2118.

Page 2

Place	Date	Hour	Summary of Events and Information	Remarks and references to Appendices
	May 19			
CROIX	12th		Routine as usual – Ceased	[illegible]
	13th		"	[illegible]
	14th		"	[illegible]
	15th		"	[illegible]
	16th		"	[illegible]
	22		6 Other Ranks proceeded to 83rd [illegible] Co at ARQUES	[illegible]
	24		Cadre entrained at CROIX for journey to DUNKIRK	[illegible]
	25		Cadre arrived at DUNKIRK	[illegible]
	30		Cadre embarked at 2.30pm at DUNKIRK on "SS CLUTHA" and after successful voyage arrived at SOUTHAMPTON the following morning	[illegible]
	31		Cadre arrived at SOUTHAMPTON 9am. After unloading the ship personnel spent the night in the rest Camps.	[illegible]
JUNE	1		Entrained at SOUTHAMPTON for DREGHORN.	[illegible]
	2		arrived DREGHORN at 7am	[illegible]
	3		majority of Personnel sent for dispersal to various stations	[illegible]
	5		All stores + mobilization equipment handed over to Ordnance	[illegible]
	6		Colour Party left Edinburgh and deposited Colours in the Officers Mess Pontefract	[illegible]

[illegible] Lt Col
[illegible]

D. D. & L., London, E.C.
(10340) Wt W5300/P713 750,000 3/18 ~~1688~~ Forms/C2118/15.

www.ingramcontent.com/pod-product-compliance
Lightning Source LLC
Chambersburg PA
CBHW080855230426
43662CB00013B/2107